Transforming Education Outcomes in Africa

Johannes Hoogeveen · Mariacristina Rossi
Editors

Transforming Education Outcomes in Africa

Learning from Togo

Editors
Johannes Hoogeveen
World Bank
Washington, DC, USA

Mariacristina Rossi
School of Management
and Economics
Università di Torino
Turin, Italy

ISBN 978-3-030-12707-7   ISBN 978-3-030-12708-4 (eBook)
https://doi.org/10.1007/978-3-030-12708-4

Library of Congress Control Number: 2019931746

© International Bank for Reconstruction and Development/The World Bank 2019, corrected publication 2019. This book is an open access publication.
The opinions expressed in this publication are those of the authors/editors and do not necessarily reflect the views of the International Bank for Reconstruction and Development/The World Bank, its Board of Directors, or the countries they represent.
Open Access This book is licensed under the terms of the Creative Commons Attribution 3.0 IGO License (https://creativecommons.org/licenses/by/3.0/igo/), which permits use, sharing, adaptation, distribution and reproduction in any medium or format, as long as you give appropriate credit to the International Bank for Reconstruction and Development/The World Bank, provide a link to the Creative Commons license and indicate if changes were made.
The use of the International Bank for Reconstruction and Development/The World Bank's name, and the use of the International Bank for Reconstruction and Development/The World Bank's logo, shall be subject to a separate written license agreement between the International Bank for Reconstruction and Development/The World Bank and the user and is not authorized as part of this CC-IGO license. Note that the link provided above includes additional terms and conditions of the license.
The images or other third party material in this book are included in the book's Creative Commons license, unless indicated otherwise in a credit line to the material. If material is not included in the book's Creative Commons license and your intended use is not permitted by statutory regulation or exceeds the permitted use, you will need to obtain permission directly from the copyright holder.
The use of general descriptive names, registered names, trademarks, service marks, etc. in this publication does not imply, even in the absence of a specific statement, that such names are exempt from the relevant protective laws and regulations and therefore free for general use.
The publisher, the authors and the editors are safe to assume that the advice and information in this book are believed to be true and accurate at the date of publication. Neither the publisher nor the authors or the editors give a warranty, expressed or implied, with respect to the material contained herein or for any errors or omissions that may have been made. The publisher remains neutral with regard to jurisdictional claims in published maps and institutional affiliations.
The World Bank does not guarantee the accuracy of the data included in this work. The boundaries, colors, denominations, and other information shown on any map in this work do not imply any judgment on the part of The World Bank concerning the legal status of any territory or the endorsement or acceptance of such boundaries.

Cover illustration: © Melisa Hasan

This Palgrave Pivot imprint is published by the registered company Springer Nature Switzerland AG
The registered company address is: Gewerbestrasse 11, 6330 Cham, Switzerland

Foreword

Every girl and every boy should have the right to a quality education so that they can have more chances in life, including employment opportunities, better health and also to participate in the political process. But education is not only a human right. Education reduces poverty, boosts economic growth, and increases income. It increases a person's chances of having a healthy life, reduces maternal deaths, and combats diseases such as HIV and AIDS. Education can promote gender equality, reduce child marriage, and promote peace. It is for this reason that education figures prominently in the Human Capital Project launched by the World Bank in 2018.

Great progress has been achieved in enrolling children in school around the world, and in Togo. The progress made is encouraging as many disparities between poor and rich, urban and rural areas and girls and boys have disappeared following the abolishment of school fees.

As this book demonstrates using a wealth of empirical data, it's not enough to get children in school. We also need to ensure that they learn to read, count, and acquire the necessary life skills. Too often this is not the case. Good teachers are essential to solving the learning crisis and closing the gap between poor and good quality education. Therefore, it is vital that all children have teachers that are well-trained, motivated, are able to identify weak learners, and are supported by well-managed education systems.

The benefits of a good education are transmitted from generation to generation and across communities at large, making investments in quality education, one of the best investments a country can make.

Identifying how to improve learning is an involved process, which needs to bring together all stakeholders. Parents, national officials, and development partners need to work closely together.

Addressing the learning crisis Togo experiences, is challenging as there are no magic bullets. Fixing education systems requires more than handing out textbooks and building schools. It requires systems to change. Good analytics as presented in this book, are a first step towards a solution. Then will follow the much more challenging step of, as the last chapter puts it, *uncovering what works trying different approaches and scaling up what works best*. Or, to put it differently: to learn how to improve learning. The journey has just begun. The World Bank is ready to play its part.

Lomé, Togo

Hawa Wague
Resident Representative for
the World Bank in Togo

The original version of the book was revised: Non-open access book has been changed to open access. The correction to the book is available at https://doi.org/10.1007/978-3-030-12708-4_6

Acknowledgements

The authors would like to thank Waly Wane, Aboudrahyme Savadogo, Pamela Mulet and an anonymous referee for their thoughtful comments and suggestions. Christopher Rockmore kindly guided us through the use of the SDI dataset; Felicien Accrombessy helped prepare summary statistics from the 2016 QUIBB. The team benefitted from discussions with Eva Bernard and the encouragement of Andrew Dabalen, Manager at the Poverty and Equity Global Practice of the World Bank.

Contents

1 **Learning in Sub-Saharan Africa** 1
Johannes Hoogeveen and Mariacristina Rossi

2 **Primary Education in Togo** 9
Johannes Hoogeveen and Mariacristina Rossi

3 **Drivers of Performance** 31
Johannes Hoogeveen, Mariacristina Rossi
and Dario Sansone

4 **Student Learning and Teacher Competence** 63
Johannes Hoogeveen, Marcello Matranga
and Mariacristina Rossi

5 **Policy Suggestions and Concluding Remarks** 87
Johannes Hoogeveen and Mariacristina Rossi

Correction to: Transforming Education Outcomes in Africa C1
Johannes Hoogeveen and Mariacristina Rossi

Index 99

NOTES ON CONTRIBUTORS

Johannes Hoogeveen is Lead Economist in the Poverty and Equity Global Practice, World Bank, USA. He has worked extensively across the Africa region, (amongst others) as country economist for Togo.

Marcello Matranga graduated from the University of Turin with a Master's degree in Economics in 2017. He is Research Assistant at CERP Collegio Carlo Alberto and Ph.D student in Economics at University of Turin, Italy. His research interests are focused on the areas of Development Economics and Economics of Education.

Mariacristina Rossi is Associate Professor at the University of Turin, Italy, and Research Affiliate at Netspar, The Netherlands; Collegio Carlo Alberto, Italy; and National Scientific Council, CNR, Italy. She has published extensively on applied development economics and intertemporal household choices.

Dario Sansone is a Ph.D. Candidate in Economics at Georgetown University, USA. He is an applied microeconomist working on labor and development. His work focuses on education and gender.

List of Figures

Fig. 1.1	Proficiency in primary education across Africa	3
Fig. 2.1	Primary school enrollment (all school types)	13
Fig. 2.2	Inequalities in school attendance (2006 and 2013/2014)	17
Fig. 2.3	Spending on primary education	18
Fig. 2.4	Number and types of classrooms and availability of books	19
Fig. 2.5	Impact of Togo's major education reforms	21
Fig. 2.6	School drop out by gender and grade in 2016/2017	22
Fig. 2.7	Performance on PASEC learning tests	23
Fig. 2.8	Percent in grade 6 performing satisfactory on PASEC learning test	24
Fig. 3.1	Primary school enrollment inequalities	34
Fig. 3.2	Primary school enrollment	34
Fig. 3.3	School characteristics: 2010–2011	35
Fig. 3.4	School performance by canton in 2010/2011 (*Note* School performance is defined as the number of students that have been admitted to participating in the primary school leaving exam over the total number of students in the school)	37
Fig. 3.5	Distribution of teachers of different grade levels by region	38
Fig. 3.6	Teacher spending per student and school performance (public schools only)	38
Fig. 3.7	Performance by school type and by region (*Note* Schools whose pass rate was equal to 0 have been dropped)	40
Fig. 3.8	Ratio of female over male students by grade in rural and urban areas (*Note* Male students are the complement to one of female student)	41

Fig. 4.1	Distribution of pupils' average scores across public (0) and private (1)	72
Fig. 4.2	Distribution of pupils' French test scores	73
Fig. 4.3	Distribution of pupils' math test scores	74
Fig. 5.1	Percent schools by percent of students that answers at least 70% of math questions correctly	89
Fig. 5.2	School attendance by socioeconomic status	90

List of Tables

Table 2.1	Changes to the primary school system	14
Table 2.2	Composition of teaching staff in public and private sector	16
Table 2.3	Internal efficiency indicators	17
Table 2.4	Budget for the education sector, 2006–2015	26
Table 3.1	Number of schools by region	39
Table 3.2	Frontier analysis for ratio of admitted CEPD students over total students in school	43
Table 3.3	Predicted school performance, by quintile and region	46
Table 3.4	Enrollment probability (6–15). Probit and Logit	49
Table 3.5	Enrollment probability (6–15)	55
Table 3.6	School achievements (6–15). Heckman	57
Table 3.7	Summary statistics	60
Table 4.1	SDI key results	65
Table 4.2	Descriptive SDI test results	71
Table 4.3	Test score correlations	74
Table 4.4	SDI test scores of pupils by region and rural and urban areas	75
Table 4.5	Distribution of teachers' test scores	76
Table 4.6	SDI test scores for teachers by region and rural and urban areas	77
Table 4.7	Analysis of variance of SDI test scores	77
Table 4.8	Summary of variables used in the regression analysis	79
Table 4.9	Regression analysis on pupils' scores	81
Table 4.10	Key SDI results for schools in Togo and selected African countries	84

LIST OF BOXES

Box 4.1 SDI test   68
Box 5.1 Community participation and school performance   91

CHAPTER 1

Learning in Sub-Saharan Africa

Johannes Hoogeveen and Mariacristina Rossi

Abstract This introductory chapter provides an overview of this book, which investigates educational outcomes in Sub-Saharan Africa with reference to one specific country: Togo.

Keywords Africa · Togo · Education · School enrollment · Learning outcomes

1.1 Introduction

Across Africa, the vision that education can be a powerful device to transform lives is widely shared. Unsurprisingly, most parents in the region will say that their priority is assuring a good education for their children. This is reflected in the results from the latest round of the World Values Survey (2010–2014): almost 80% of African parents responded to be worried or very worried about their ability to give their children a good education.

J. Hoogeveen (✉)
World Bank, Washington, DC, USA
e-mail: jhoogeveen@worldbank.org

M. Rossi
School of Management and Economics, Università di Torino, Turin, Italy
e-mail: mariacristina.rossi@unito.it

© International Bank for Reconstruction
and Development/The World Bank 2019
J. Hoogeveen and M. Rossi (eds.), *Transforming Education Outcomes in Africa*, https://doi.org/10.1007/978-3-030-12708-4_1

The importance given to education by parents is echoed in the economics literature, which finds that a country's education level is critical for its economic success. For many years, this literature focused on the positive effects of the quantity of education on growth (Barro 1991; Mankiw et al. 1992). Also, in practice much effort goes into assuring that every child has the opportunity to attend school. Driven in large part by the Millennium Development Goal of achieving a 100% primary completion by 2015, many countries in Africa put in place policies that abolished school fees and assured free and universal primary education. These efforts have largely been successful, at times extremely successful. In Uganda, for instance, the removal of direct costs to schooling increased primary enrollment by over 60% and lowered cost-related dropouts by over 33 percentage points (Deininger 2003). The expansion of schooling across the continent is remarkable in its scope and speed. Was in 1970 the gross primary enrollment rate in Sub-Saharan Africa 68%, presently it is over 100%. Average years of schooling of people aged 15 and over increased from 3.89 in 1990 to 5.23 by 2010. Over the same period, those with no schooling at all dropped from 44 to 32% (Barro and Lee 2013).

More recently a growing body of evidence suggests it is not only the *quantity* of schooling, measured by average years of schooling or enrollment rates but also the *quality* of schooling, proxied by student achievement tests, that contributes to growth. Enrollment, despite being the first step, is not equivalent to education. Enrollment alone is not enough to generate sufficient knowledge capital that economies need to grow. Education needs to equip each child with adequate competencies in literacy, numeracy and science. It is not about being in school but what is learned in school that matters (Hanushek and Kimko 2000; Pritchett 2001; Hanushek and Woessmann 2007, 2012).

Unfortunately, there is often a trade-off between going to school and learning. Particularly when enrollment rates increase rapidly, learning outcomes tend to suffer. In a recent paper, Hoogeveen and Rossi (2013) showed for Tanzania that the impact of the introduction of free primary education school reform had a negative impact on grade achievements. The results also point at an unequal effect, as the negative impact was particularly marked for those living in rural areas and originating from poor families. Perhaps unsurprisingly in view of the rapid expansion of Africa's primary education system, learning outcomes are increasingly of

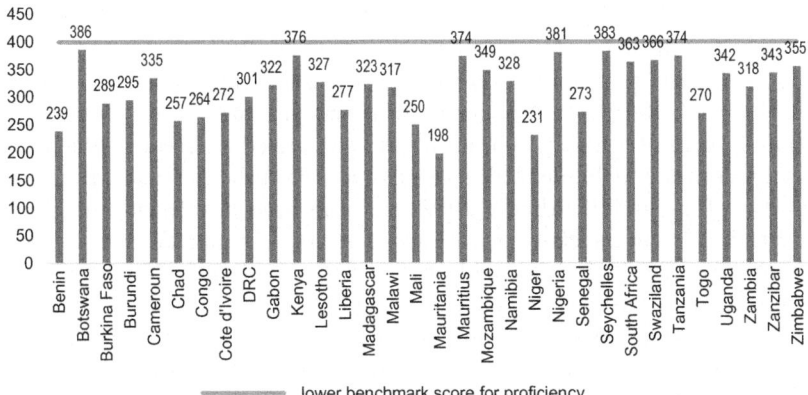

Fig. 1.1 Proficiency in primary education across Africa (*Source* Authors' calculations using the Altinok et al. data base)

concern (Bashir et al. 2018). Evidence from the global dataset on education quality compiled by Altinok et al. (2017) demonstrates the degree to which African primary school systems perform unsatisfactorily. Across the region, school systems are unable to meet the lower bar for proficiency, set at a score of 400. The higher benchmark of intermediate proficiency (set at 475) is entirely out of reach, even though it is achieved in Central and Eastern Asia, Europe and North America. Within sub-Saharan Africa there are large differences, however. With an average score of 253, francophone West Africa performs worse than the remainder of the region that has an average score of 331; within francophone West Africa Togo does better than the average with a score of 270 (Figure 2.8 suggests this is driven by Togo's performance on mathematics and not by proficiency in French for which Togo trails countries in the sub-region)[1] (Fig. 1.1).

The consequences of such low learning outcomes are severe. According to the Brookings Institution's Center for Universal Education, and drawing data from its Africa Learning Barometer,[2] 61 million children (half of the primary school-age population) "will reach their adolescent years without being able to read, write or perform basic numeracy tasks." Their study identified 12 countries in Africa, namely,

---

[1] The Altinok et al. dataset does not include the data from the latest SACMEQ III round, so for a recent comparison across the subregion, the reader should refer to Fig. 2.8.

[2] http://www.brookings.edu/research/interactives/africa-learning-barometer.

Malawi, Zambia, Ivory Coast, Ghana, Benin, Nigeria, Chad, Ethiopia, Congo, South Africa, Namibia and Comoros in which not even 30% of children meet the minimum standard of learning by grade five of primary school. But the consequences of poor education go much beyond limited learning. Quality education has been linked to better labor market outcomes and higher levels of income (Hanushek et al. 2017), less poverty (Jung and Thorbecke 2003) and improved health and nutrition. It has also been associated with lower fertility, less inequality, a smaller probability of incarceration and even a higher propensity for happiness (Cuñado and de Gracia 2012).

This book delves deeper into questions of enrollment and learning outcomes. In particular, it asks the question what, given increased enrollment rates, a country can do to bring its learning outcomes up to standard. We explore the scope for improvements, by enhancing the efficiency with which resources are used, by improving the qualifications of teachers but also through greater community involvement in school management. We find that there is certainly scope for improvement. Yet we conclude that changes at the margin will be insufficient to bring about the transformation that is needed to not only achieve intermediate proficiency levels but to go beyond this and attain intermediate proficiency levels. What could be done to transform the education system is discussed in the last chapter.

The focus of this book is on one country, Togo. By picking one country we are able to go into greater depth. Togo was selected because the challenges its education system faces are broadly comparable to those in other education systems in sub-Saharan Africa. The choice of Togo was facilitated by the fact that a broad range of micro data is available, including household surveys, learning surveys as well as detailed administrative data on budgets and the school system. We draw on these data for this book.

The rest of this book is laid out as follows. Chapter 2 gives an overview of the educational system and outcomes in Togo. Chapter 3 uses an efficiency frontier approach and examines the regional differences in educational outcomes in Togo. Chapter 4 illustrates the determinants of children's learning outcomes using survey data by including information on school characteristics and teacher proficiency. Conclusions follow in Chapter 5.

Appendix

Data Used in This Study

Several datasets are going to be used in the remainder of this book. In addition to PASEC, which covers learning by pupils in grade two and five of primary school children, we will make use of selected years of the school census containing data for all schools. This administrative data set contains much information on schools itself but lacks information on the demand side, i.e. characteristics of the household from which the students originate. From this dataset a pronounced heterogeneity stands out. The best performing schools are private schools; Kara, Lomé and the Central region are the regions with the highest levels of performance. There is also a clear gender dimension in school performances, which suggests that in all regions and across all school types boys perform better than girls, in contrast to the OECD evidence which shows opposite direction. Results will be shown in Chapter 3. In this chapter we also make use of survey data, QUIBB, to relate school performance to household characteristics and control for wealth indicators. The survey data refer to 2006 and 2011 and contain 7500 interviewed households during the first wave, including 36,430 individuals, whereas 5532 households and 29,781 individuals took part to the second wave. These cross-sectional datasets are extremely useful for the purpose of our research as they provide information on household composition, education, health, employment, assets, current expenditure, autoconsumption and income. Moreover, the dataset contains school attendance in the past week rather than school enrollment as in the administrative data, shedding light on the actual decision on going to school rather than being (merely) enrolled. In Chapter 4, we make use of survey data complementary to PASEC, the SDI data, which focus on pupils in their fourth grade. SDI data contain, in addition to pupils' data, information on teachers' such as their working history as well as their knowledge in math and French.

References

Altinok, Nadir, Noam Angrist, and Harry Patrinos. 2017. A Global Dataset on Education Quality (1965–2015). World Bank Policy Research Working Paper No. 8314.

Barro, Robert J. 1991. Economic Growth in a Cross Section of Countries. *The Quarterly Journal of Economics* 106 (2): 407–443.
Barro, Robert J., and Jong Wha Lee. 2013. A New Data Set of Educational Attainment in the World, 1950–2010. *Journal of Development Economics* 104 (2013): 184–198.
Bashir, Sajitha, Marlaine Lockheed, Elizabeth Ninan, and Jee-Peng Tan. 2018. *Facing Forward: Schooling for Learning in Africa*. Africa Development Forum Series. Washington, DC: World Bank. https://doi.org/10.1596/978-1-46481260-6.
Cuñado, J., and F.P. de Gracia. 2012. Does Education Affect Happiness? Evidence for Spain. *Social Indicators Research* 108: 185–196. https://doi.org/10.1007/s11205-011-9874-x.
Deininger, Klaus. 2003. Does Cost of Schooling Affect Enrollment by the Poor? Universal Primary Education in Uganda. *Economics of Education Review* 22 (3): 291–305.
Hanushek, E.A., and D.D. Kimko. 2000. Schooling, Labor-Force Quality, and the Growth of Nations. *American Economic Review* 90 (5): 1184–1208.
Hanushek, E.A., and L. Woessmann. 2007. The Role of Education Quality in Economic Growth. World Bank Policy Research Working Paper, 4122, Washington, DC.
Hanushek, E.A., and L. Woessmann. 2012. Do Better School Lead to More Growth? Cognitive Skills, Economic Outcomes, and Causation. *Journal of Economic Growth* 17 (4): 267–321.
Hanushek, Eric A., Guido Schwerdt, Ludger Woessmann, and Lei Zhang. 2017. General Education, Vocational Education, and Labor-Market Outcomes Over the Lifecycle. *Journal of Human Resources* 52 (1): 48–87.
Hoogeveen, Johannes, and Mariacristina Rossi. 2013. Enrollment and Grade Attainment Following the Introduction of Free Primary Education in Tanzania. *Journal of African Economies* 22 (3): 375–393.
Jung, Hong-Sang, and Erik Thorbecke. 2003. The Impact of Public Education Expenditure on Human Capital, Growth, and Poverty in Tanzania and Zambia: A General Equilibrium Approach. *Journal of Policy Modeling* 25 (8): 701–725.
Mankiw, N. Gregory, David Romer, and David N. Weil. 1992. A Contribution to the Empirics of Economic Growth. *The Quarterly Journal of Economics* 107 (2): 407–437.
Pritchett, Lant. 2001. Where Has All the Education Gone? *World Bank Economic Review* 15 (3): 367–391.

The opinions expressed in this chapter are those of the author(s) and do not necessarily reflect the views of the International Bank for Reconstruction and Development/The World Bank, its Board of Directors, or the countries they represent.

Open Access This chapter is licensed under the terms of the Creative Commons Attribution 3.0 IGO License (https://creativecommons.org/licenses/by/3.0/igo/), which permits use, sharing, adaptation, distribution and reproduction in any medium or format, as long as you give appropriate credit to the International Bank for Reconstruction and Development/The World Bank, provide a link to the Creative Commons license and indicate if changes were made.

The use of the International Bank for Reconstruction and Development/The World Bank's name, and the use of the International Bank for Reconstruction and Development/The World Bank's logo, shall be subject to a separate written license agreement between the International Bank for Reconstruction and Development/The World Bank and the user and is not authorized as part of this CC-IGO license. Note that the link provided above includes additional terms and conditions of the license.

The images or other third party material in this chapter are included in the chapter's Creative Commons license, unless indicated otherwise in a credit line to the material. If material is not included in the chapter's Creative Commons license and your intended use is not permitted by statutory regulation or exceeds the permitted use, you will need to obtain permission directly from the copyright holder.

CHAPTER 2

Primary Education in Togo

Johannes Hoogeveen and Mariacristina Rossi

Abstract This chapter offers an overview of primary education in Togo, spanning the two last decades. Togo made important progress. School enrollment increased considerably and the percentage of school-aged children not attending school dropped significantly. At the same time, learning outcomes give reason for concern as the quality of education appears to be wanting. This challenge is not specific to Togo; it affects other African school systems as well though its seriousness varies from country to country.

Keywords School enrollment · Learning outcomes · Togo · Free primary education

J. Hoogeveen (✉)
World Bank, Washington, DC, USA
e-mail: jhoogeveen@worldbank.org

M. Rossi
School of Management and Economics, Università di Torino, Turin, Italy
e-mail: mariacristina.rossi@unito.it

2.1 Primary Education Since the Year 2000

Togo is a sovereign state in West Africa bordered by Ghana to the west, Benin to the east and Burkina Faso to the north. It extends south to the Gulf of Guinea, where its capital Lomé is located. Togo covers 57,000 square kilometers making it one of the smallest countries in Africa and has a population of less than 8 million. The country has known a long period of economic decline and political upheaval that started in the early 1990s and which formally ended with the parliamentary elections of October 2007. The education sector suffered greatly during this period. Financial constraints prevented the renewal and upgrading of the teaching profession and the renovation or construction of education facilities at a pace sufficient to meet constantly growing needs for education.

With the limited spending of the public sector in education and as the crisis deepened, parents responded by sending their children to private schools. So, while between 2000 and 2005 the number of students attending public primary school increased by 5%, the number of students going to private schools (for profit and religious establishments, but also local initiative schools referred to in French as *École d'Initiative Locale* (EDIL)) increased by 20%. Nationwide, 40% of students attended a private–public school in 2000; by 2005 this had increased to 43%. In rural areas one saw a proliferation of EDIL schools, which relied entirely on local community financing and family support. The importance of private education is illustrated by the fact that in the year 2000 more than half the schools in the Savanes, one of the poorest regions of the country, were non-public 43% were of the EDIL type; another 17% were private schools. While in other rural areas public provision continued to be more important than private provision, in urban areas private provision outstripped public provision as well. In the year 2000 but also in 2010 the proportion of urban students enrolled in private institutions was around 66%.[1]

As donor support was withdrawn during the crisis the public education sector relied entirely on financing by the State. Capital spending was reduced, hiring was limited and the education system started to rely more on so-called contract teachers—temporary and auxiliary teachers who work for a fraction of the wages of civil servants but who are also

---

[1] Of these few attended EDIL schools as this kinds of school is almost exclusively found in rural areas.

less qualified (UNESCO, UNICEF 2014). These developments explain, as will be demonstrated later, why the quality of education declined so rapidly during this period.

Parents had good reason to opt for private alternatives as the quality of public education was deteriorating as evidenced by the fact that even though the number of students increased in public schools, the number of teachers declined by 12%, resulting in rising student–teacher ratios (from 1:36 in 2000 to 1:43 in 2005). On a positive note the teachers that left tended to be those with less education themselves, those with a primary or secondary school diploma, while the number of teachers with a baccalaureate increased. As a consequence, the ratio of teachers with only a primary or secondary school diplomas decreased from 80 to 75%. In private (non-EDIL) schools, the increase in teachers kept pace with the increase in students and student–teacher ratios remained constant at 1:32. In private schools too, teacher qualifications went up, in a way that was more pronounced than in public schools. Had in 2000 some 75% a primary or secondary school diploma, by 2005 this percentage had dropped to less than 50%.

During the crisis years, Togo's citizens thus demonstrated to value education. Remarkably throughout the years of economic hardship enrollment levels remained high in comparison with most other West African countries. In fact, they even increased. The net primary school enrollment rate for children aged 6–11 years rose from 63% in 2000 to 73% in 2006 and the gross rate for the same age group increased from 103 to 115%.

Encouraged by the success of the 2007 elections and the new government's reform platform, which included the abolition of school fees starting in the 2008/2009 school year and the gradual integration of EDIL schools in the public school system, donors reengaged with the country after more than 15 years of providing limited assistance. By 2010 an strategic Education Sector Plan (PSE) had been formulated and adopted and money from external education financiers started flowing again.[2]

Following the introduction of free primary education, enrollment rates increased rapidly. Additional teachers were hired and by 2016 the number of public school teachers had almost doubled from 14,000 in 2006 to over 24,000. As student numbers increased in lock-step,

---

[2] A free-fee education policy was already established in the 1992 Constitution, but remained unimplemented. In 2000, tuition fees for girls were reduced, to encourage their enrollment, and in 2007–2008, all primary-school fees were abolished.

student–teacher ratios did not change, and remained at 1:43. The education background of teachers did improve however and the fraction of teachers with a primary or secondary school diploma dropped to 62%. As public-primary education became free, the number of students attending private schools stabilized at around 450,000 students, while the share of students attending private schools dropped to 30% in 2016—down from 43% a decade earlier. Unlike in public schools the qualifications of private-school teachers did not improve further and the student–teacher ratio, though still favorable relative to public schools, increased to 1:34 (up from 1:32 a decade earlier).

Not only did more children receive an education, the new policies of absorbing EDIL schools in the public school system and abolishing school fees were pro-poor as the children that benefited most originated from the poorest households in rural areas. And as more children were going to school (net enrollment reached 94% in 2016/2017), other, spatial and gender, inequalities reduced as well.

Remarkably for a system that had to deal with a large influx of new students and the absorption of EDIL schools, internal efficiency also went up: many more children passed their primary school leaver exam and fewer children repeated their grade or dropped out completely. So, in almost all respects the education reforms initiated in 2007 were a resounding success. The number of children who completed primary school doubled over the course of a decade, an increase that was achieved while improving the efficiency of the education system and without affecting pass rates in any negative way. If anything, a larger fraction of children was successful at their exam.

2.2 Closer Look at the Introduction of Free Primary Education

Togo's educational system is divided into four levels: (i) a three-year pre-school cycle designed for 3–5 year olds; (ii) a six-year primary cycle designed for 6–11 year olds; (iii) a seven-year secondary education cycle designed for 12–18 year olds, consisting of a four-year junior level and a three-year senior level and (iv) a higher education system. There is also technical and vocational training at the junior and senior secondary levels and literacy training. The focus of this book is on the six-year primary cycle, which can be sub-divided into three groups: CP1 and CP2, the

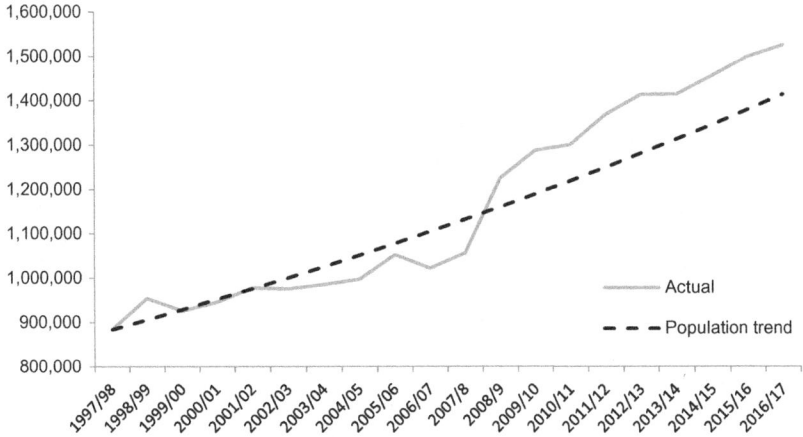

Fig. 2.1 Primary school enrollment (all school types) (*Source* Authors' calculations using Government of Togo, National Yearbooks of School Statistics. Various years)

first two years, CE1 and CE2, years three and four, and CM1 and CM2, years five and six. At the end of year six, students sit for an end of school exam, the CPED.

Prior to the start of the 2008/2009 school year, which normally runs from September till June the following year, the Government of Togo announced it would abolish school fees for primary education. After a decade of slow growth in which increases in enrollment remained below the population growth trend, the introduction of free primary education led to a rapid increase in enrollment. The biggest increase was registered during the first year primary education was free, after which followed a period in which primary school enrollment largely kept pace with population growth (Fig. 2.1). The inflow of new students came as a shock to the system. Between 2006/2007 and 2008/2009 the number of students attending public primary school increased from 590,000 to 777,000 a 32% increase. In the course of 2 years, 500 new schools and 2300 teachers were absorbed into the public education system, an increase of 19 respectively 17%. Not all these schools were newly constructed, nor were all additional teachers new hires. Some 228 newly incorporated schools were former EDIL schools that were now absorbed into the public school system along with their students and teachers.

Table 2.1 Changes to the primary school system

	Schools (%)		Classrooms (%)		Students (%)		Teachers (%)	
	2006/2007	2016/2017	2006/2007	2016/2017	2006/2007	2016/2017	2006/2007	2016/2017
Public	47	68	52	66	58	70	51	64
Catholic	11	8	11	8	12	8	12	8
Protestant	4	4	4	4	4	4	4	4
Islamic	1	1	0	1	0	1	1	2
Private laic	17	17	18	20	13	17	18	21
EDIL	21	2	13	1	12	1	14	1
Total	100	100	100	100	100	100	100	100
Total	5586	7315	26,321	37,495	1,021,617	1,524,195	26,103	37,985

Source Authors' calculations using Government of Togo, National Yearbooks of School Statistics. Various Years

Table 2.1 illustrates the changes the primary school system went through with the introduction of free primary education. To this end we compare the school system in the year shortly before the reforms were introduced (2006/2007) with the system 10 years later. Over the course of a decade, the number of students increased by almost 50% from one million, to a million and a half. Schools became bigger on average as the number of schools increased by less than the increase in the number of students: 31%. Also, the number of students per classroom and the number of students per teacher increased, though not by much as the number of classrooms increased by 42% and the number of teachers by 46%.

As one might expect, the share of students going to public schools increased. Surprisingly, though, this increase did not come at the expense of private (religious and non-religious) schools which, unlike public schools did not abolish school fees. The increase in the fraction of students going to public schools is largely the results of EDIL schools being absorbed in the public school system. Noteworthy is that amongst the private schools, Catholic schools became less popular. Private non-religious schools picked up the students that stopped going to Catholic schools.

As teaching staff is a critical input into education, it is worth considering how its composition evolved before and after the introduction of free primary education. Of note is that both in public and private schools the number of teachers increased substantially. Moreover, within the public school system there is a strong weakness due to the composition of teachers with respect to their contract and payment. The public system relies more substantially than the private one on teaching assistants/volunteers and temporary staff, staff who tend to get paid half or less than half, compared to what their civil servant colleagues make.[3] In private education establishments such staff made up more than 10% of the total staff complement in 2006/2007 and in 2016/2017 only 2%. Compare this to the public school system where half the teachers are assistants or people with temporary contracts. The private school system also increased the fraction of female staff, from 14% in 2006/2007 to 21% in 2016/2017. In the public sector little changed: female teachers make up some 14% of the total teaching complement (Table 2.2).

---

[3] Temporary teachers are in their probationary period and will either be confirmed as civil servants or dismissed. Their earnings are lower than civil servants. Assistant/volunteer teachers are individuals who do not have the necessary qualifications to be recruited as temps and therefore work as assistants in hopes of being integrated to the civil service rolls at a later date. These individuals earned less than 5000 FCFA/month ($10) in 2013.

Table 2.2 Composition of teaching staff in public and private sector

Public	Total	Civil servant (%)	Assistant (%)	Temp (%)	Private (%)	Male (%)	Female (%)
2006/2007	13,290	42	40	18	0	87	13
2016/2017	24,490	40	37	23	0	86	14
Private							
2006/2007	9060	16	5	4	75	86	14
2016/2017	13,178	12	2	0	85	79	21

Source Authors' calculations using Government of Togo, National Yearbooks of School Statistics. Various Years

Such major reforms come with growing pains, if only because all of a sudden, a large cohort of students entered CP1. Between 2006/2007 and 2008/2009 the number of children in public school CP1 increased from 127,000 to 208,000, a 64% increase. As this bulge of students worked itself through the primary school system, the situation gradually normalized in subsequent years. Consequently, four years later, in 2012/2013, the number of students in CP1 was 139,000. Student–teacher ratios, already high at 44.4 students per teacher in 2006/2007 increased to 49.7 two years later and returned to 44.4 by 2012/2013.

Despite the stresses under which the education system was put, the system's internal efficiency improved across the board. In its wake, almost all gender disparities were eliminated as well. The fraction of six-year-old children attending school increased significantly, especially after 2012. The fraction of pupils not passing to the next grade declined dramatically from almost one in four between 2006 and 2008 to one in thirteen by 2016/2017 following the adoption of a decree at the beginning of the 2012/2013 school year which limited the ability of schools to let pupils repeat grades. Also the number of pupils who abandoned school dropped (Table 2.3).

The increase in enrollment reduced inequalities. Poverty in Togo broadly follows a north–south axis with poverty being worst in the north and lower in the south. Like poverty, and before the abolition of primary school fees, attendance rates in regions in northern Togo (Savanes and Kara) were much lower than elsewhere in the country. This can be illustrated with survey data, showing that in 2006 attendance rates in the northern regions were as low as 52% in 2006 in Savanes. By 2013/2014 attendance rates in this region had increased by 25% age points to 77%. As a consequence the gap with the best performing region (Lomé) reduced from 40% in 2006 to 12% in 2013/2014. The large increase in school enrollment and attendance turned out to be a great equalizer.

Table 2.3 Internal efficiency indicators

	2006/2007	2007/2008	2012/2013	2016/2017
Children aged 6 attending school				
Girls	46.5	47.0	54.8	72.6
Boys	49.6	50.3	56.0	72.9
Percent of pupils not passing to the next grade				
Girls	23.4	24.0	18.6	7.6
Boys	22.8	23.3	18.4	7.7
Percent of pupils who started but did not complete primary school				
Girls		38.0	38.5	30.4
Boys		24.1	34.4	30.2

Source Government of Togo, National Yearbook of School Statistics, for 2012/2013 and 2016/2017 and PASEC 2012 for 2006/2007 and 2007/2008

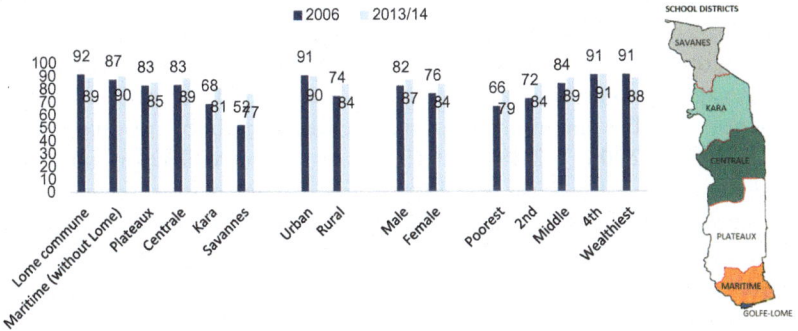

Fig. 2.2 Inequalities in school attendance (2006 and 2013/2014) (*Source* 2006 data—MICS; 2013/2014 data—DHS)

Girls caught up relatively to boys, children living in poor households reduced the gap relative to those living in better-off households as did those living in rural areas. Inequalities did not fully disappear, but by 2013/2014, five years after introducing free primary education, they had reduced considerably as the difference between the best (Lomé) and the worst (Savanes) performing region dropped from 40 to 18%, between rural and urban areas from 17 to 6% and between the poorest and wealthiest quintile from 25 to 9% (Fig. 2.2).

A decade after the introduction of free primary education, in 2017, almost 100,000 children in public primary school successfully completed their primary school leaver exam. Some 130,000 pupils sat for the exam, implying a success rate of 77%. This was a remarkable achievement, as over the course of a decade the number of students who successfully completed primary school had effectively doubled. In 2006/2007 49,000 passed the CEPD exam out of 71,000 who sat for it, a pass rate of 69%. As pass rates improved, they improved more for girls whose likelihood of passing improved from 64 to 75%, than for boys (from 71 to 78%). These achievements are even more remarkable when one realizes that not only pass rates improved, students arrived in grade 6 faster as grade repetition rates had reduced remarkably. Where in 2006/2007 one in four children repeated their grade, a decade later this had dropped to less than 10%.

Such a reform effort does not come cheap. In fact, between 2006 and 2015 the budget for primary education almost quadrupled from FCFA 14 billion in 2006 to FCFA 56 billion in 2015. So while the number of public students almost doubled during that period, real spending per student increased as well, by as much as nearly 80% from FCFA 23,000 to FCFA 43,000. This was possible, in part, because during this period the economy of Togo recovered from crisis levels. GDP growth became positive again and revenue collection improved considerably. Expressed as a fraction of GDP spending on primary education almost doubled from 1.3 of GDP in 2006 to 2.4% in 2015, but as revenue collection improved rapidly following the crisis the increase as expressed in percent of the budget was less (from 5.6% in 2006 to 6.8% in 2015). In fact, for most of the period the share of primary education in public spending remained relatively constant hovering around 7% of revenue collected (Fig. 2.3).

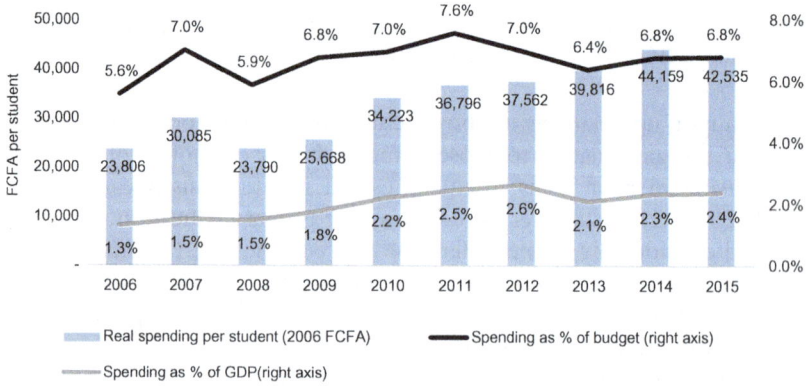

Fig. 2.3 Spending on primary education (*Source* Authors' calculations using Government of Togo, National Yearbooks of School Statistics. Various years)

As spending increased a sector that had neglected investments during the crisis years, ramped up. The investment budget increased by a factor 8 from around FCFA 2 billion in 2008 to more than 16 billion in 2011, a level at which it remained for the next 3 years, before starting to taper off in 2014 (see Annex Table 2.4). As a result, the total number of classrooms increased from 22,272 in 2009 to 24,926 in 2016, while a number of classrooms made from stamped earth were converted into more permanent materials. Despite these investments, considerable regional differences in the type of construction materials used for schools continued to persist: particularly in the poorer regions of Plateaux and

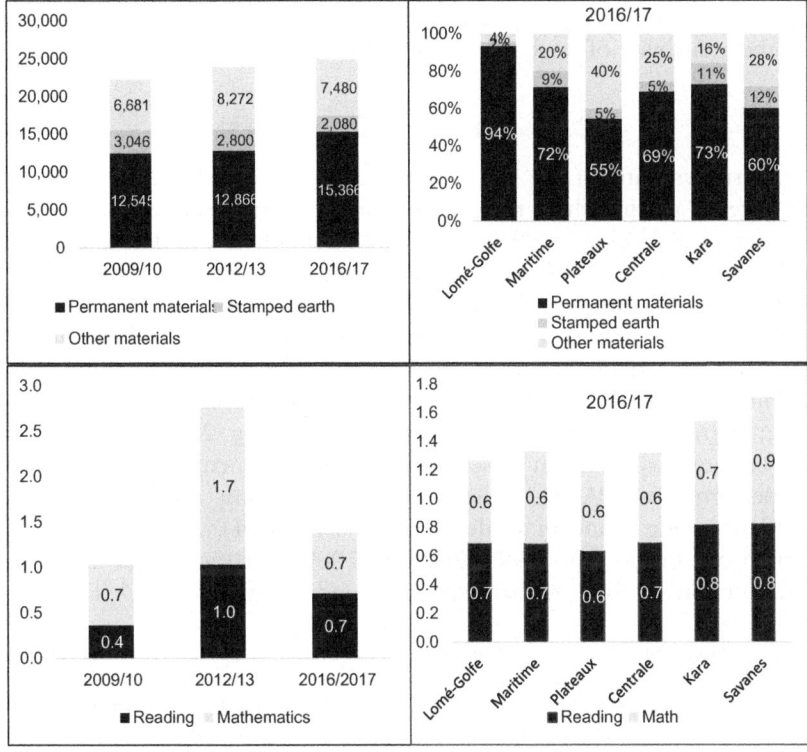

Fig. 2.4 Number and types of classrooms and availability of books (*Source* Authors' calculations using Government of Togo, National Yearbooks of School Statistics. Various years)

Savanes the fraction of schools constructed out of permanent materials tends to be low. These are the same regions were in the past the highest number of EDIL schools were found. And as such schools tended to be community-financed, the majority of these schools were constructed from less permanent materials (Fig. 2.4).

The story for the availability of text books at school also points to significant improvements—at least initially. These improvements came on the back of a large joint Government and donor effort to ensure that at least every student had one book for maths and one book for reading. This effort was largely successful as evidenced by the data for 2012/2013, a year in which 3 million text free books were distributed, but its effects seem to be petering out. One positive aspect to note is that in Savanes, the poorest and usually most underserved region in the country the availability of textbooks is highest (Fig. 2.5).

2.3 Learning Outcomes

While success rates at the school leaver exam improved, not all students advance to a stage where they can sit for the school leaver exam. Dropout rates remain elevated. Almost one in five children quit during or after their first year at school. Of those who remain, most make it till grade 5 (CM1) when another 10% drops out. All in all, of every 100 children starting primary school, only 70 complete it. This number is the same for boys and for girls, but there is a marked difference when they drop out. During the first year of school, boys have a bigger likelihood of dropping; in grade 5 girls are more likely to drop out (Fig. 2.6).

For those who remain in school learning assessments show a decline in performance. PASEC collects data on learning achievements for pupils in grade 2 and in grade 5 (grade 6 in 2014). Assessments were carried out in the years 1999/2000, in 2009/2010, one year after the introduction of free primary education and in 2013/2014.[4] The first

---

[4]The "Programme d'Analyse des Systèmes Éducatifs" (PASEC, or "Programme of Analysis of Education Systems") was launched by the Conference of Ministers of Education of French-Speaking Countries (CONFEMEN). These surveys are conducted in French-speaking countries in Sub-Saharan Africa in primary school (grade 2 and 5) for Mathematics and French. Each round includes ten countries. PASEC I occurred from 1996 to 2003; PASEC II from 2004 to 2010 and PASEC III was conducted in 2014. The PASEC assessment tools evolved over time, and the raw PASEC score are not comparable. Yet each PASEC round defines a cut-off score above which performance may be considered satisfactory. We use the percent performing satisfactory in each round to make comparisons, whereby we use the PASEC score obtained by the end-of-the year test for year when PASEC also carried out a test at the beginning of the school year.

2 PRIMARY EDUCATION IN TOGO   21

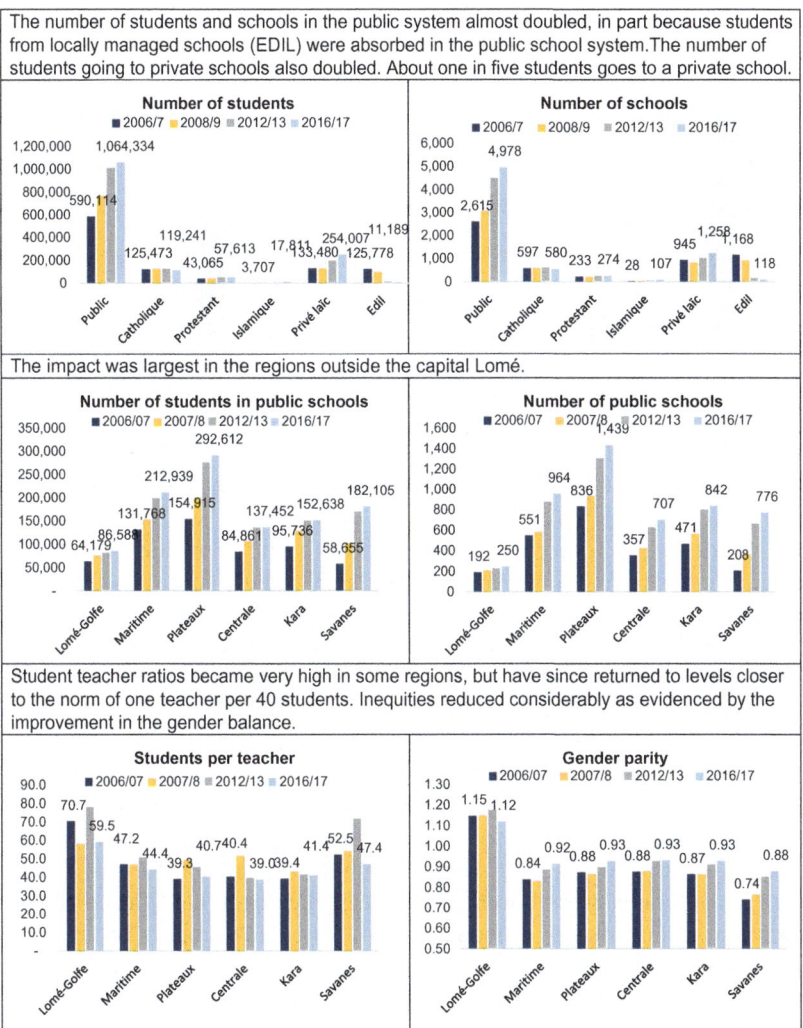

Fig. 2.5 Impact of Togo's major education reforms (*Source* Government of Togo, National Yearbook of School Statistics. Various years)

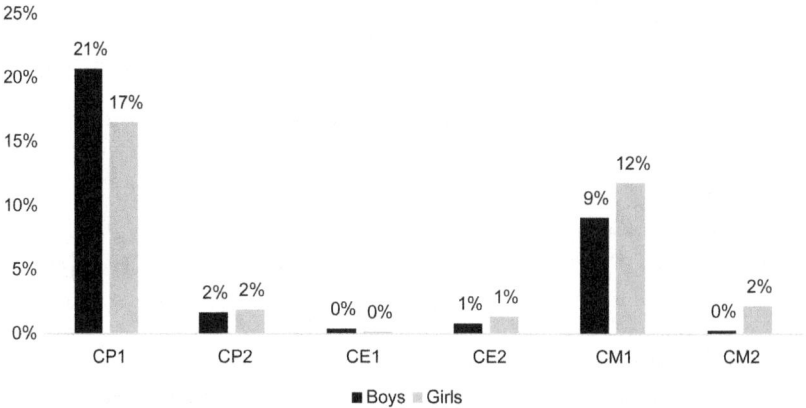

Fig. 2.6 School drop out by gender and grade in 2016/2017 (*Source* Government of Togo, National Yearbook of School Statistics, 2016/2017)

assessment implemented nine years prior to the introduction of free primary education was introduced, finds that the majority of students in grade 2 and grade 5 performed satisfactory on both the French and mathematics tests. This changed in the second round implemented in 2009/2010. Now the majority of students whether in second or in fifth grade are no longer performing adequately. Only 40% of students in grade 2 perform satisfactory on the French test, and even less (29%) in grade 5. The latter is remarkable as students in grade 2 are part of large cohort of students who benefited from free primary education. Hence given the stress the arrival of large numbers of additional students in CP1 put on the education system, one might expect that for this cohort learning outcomes were lower. Indeed, evidence from e.g. Tanzania suggests that large influxes of students have a negative impact on learning achievement (Hoogeveen and Rossi 2013). What the Togo data show is that this negative impact spilled over to students in other grades, even though they started their education career prior to the introduction of free primary education. One possible explanation for this is that as a large body of new students entered the school system, classrooms and teachers initially assigned to higher grades were reassigned to CP1 to accommodate the new students. This is supported by the evolution of student to classroom ratios which increased between 2000 and 2010 from 40 to 53 for students in grade 2—is expected as this is the cohort with additional

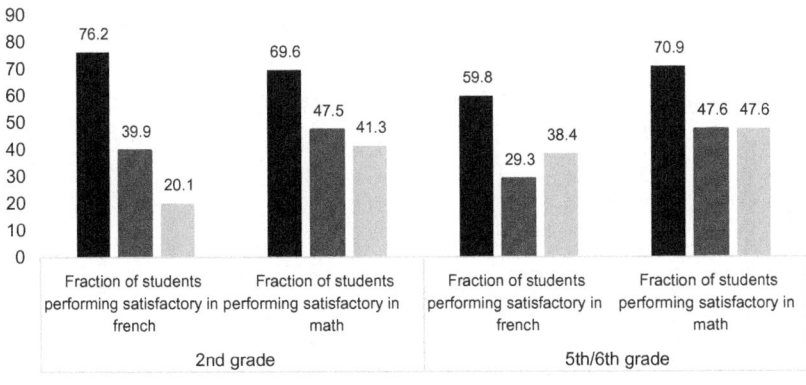

Fig. 2.7 Performance on PASEC learning tests (*Source* PASEC Country Reports for Togo, 2012 and 2014)

free education students, but also increased for students in grade 5: from 37 to 52 students per classroom. Another, complementary explanation is that the economic and political crisis left its mark on the quality of education in Togo's primary schools, reducing learning across the board.

Learning wise, the education system appears not to have recovered from the shock and in 2014 student PASEC scores are more or less comparable with those from 2010. They are worse for students in grade 2 for which the fraction of students that performs satisfactory dropped even further, and compare (math) or worse (French) for students in grade 5 (Fig. 2.7).

2.4 Is Togo a Special Case?

The experience of Togo is illustrative for what happened elsewhere in low income sub-Saharan Africa (i.e. countries with per capita incomes of less $1000). Like Togo, most countries substantially increased primary school enrollment. For the 24 low-income countries in the region, net enrollment went up from 55% in 2000 to 76% in 2016 (Togo went from 51 to 89%). Despite the increase in enrollment, inequities continue to exist in Togo, by gender (90% male; 87% female), by location (96% urban; 85% rural) and particularly by wealth class (80% poorest quintile; 97% wealthiest quintile). These patterns are not dissimilar to those found elsewhere in the region.

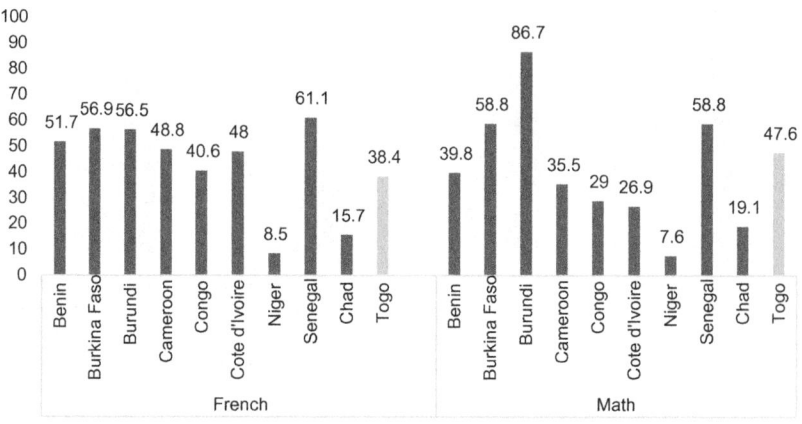

Fig. 2.8 Percent in grade 6 performing satisfactory on PASEC learning test (*Source* PASEC Country Report for Togo, 2014)

Also, with respect to the outcomes on the learning tests does Togo not stand out relative to comparators in francophone Africa. Looking across PASEC test results for francophone countries one notes that Togo performs better than some (Chad and Niger in particular) and worse than others (Senegal, Burundi, Burkina Faso). Togo does worse in French than most francophone countries, and better in maths. In fact, Togo performs pretty much around the average score which is 42.7 for French and 41.0 for maths. Like other countries the problem of low learning achievement emerges in the early grades (Bashir et al. 2018) (Fig. 2.8).

2.5 Conclusion to the Chapter

Viewed from one perspective, Togo's education system has been remarkably successful. During the economic and political crisis that affected the country between the mid-1990s and early 2000s, Togolese parents continued to make sure their children enrolled in primary schools, often opting for private education or resorting to community initiatives. Following the crisis, the public system recovered and navigated successfully the stresses associated with the abolishment of school fees. Its introduction starting in the 2008/2009 school year led to a rapid expansion of the primary school system, which was aptly managed.

Student–teacher and student–classroom ratios increased, but only temporarily as more teachers were recruited and more classrooms constructed. Pass rates improved and the system managed to enhance its internal efficiency, reducing the fraction of students that do not pass from one grade to the next and limiting school drop out. As many more students started attending school, many—though not all, of the disparities between regions, rural and urban areas, by gender and wealth categories disappeared.

Free primary education did not come without cost and the Togolese authorities allocated substantial budgetary resources to primary education, in fact more than doubling the percent of GDP spent on primary education. Also spending per pupil increased considerably. These achievements demonstrate the commitment of Togolese parents and authorities to education.

Yet there is another perspective. Expanding access, improving attendance, enhancing efficiency and providing budgetary resources alone, is not sufficient to guarantee success. Too many children continue to drop out of school, implying individual drama and resource wastage. More importantly, evidence from learning tests suggests that the majority of primary school leavers do not master core competencies in reading, writing, and arithmetic. The results are suggestive of a profound learning crisis.

So it happened that the number of students in the public primary school system doubled from 570,000 in 2000 to over a million in 2014, and that the number of students who completed primary school went up from 100,000 in 2000 to around 200,000 in 2014. Yet, though budgets more than doubled (expressed in real terms they went up by a factor 2.35), the number of students who left primary school performing satisfactory in French increased only from 71,000 in 2000 to about 95,000 in 2014. The number of students performing satisfactory in math increased less, from about 60,000 in 2000 to 77,000 in 2014. Expressed this way, the enormous increase in spending appears to have achieved little.

Both school attendance and learning while at school are needed to assure that money invested in education yields a decent return. It is not the case now, which raises the question what could be done to rectify the situation. This question is explored in the remainder of this book.

Annex

See Table 2.4.

Table 2.4 Budget for the education sector, 2006–2015

	2006	2007	2008	2009	2010	2011	2012	2013	2014	2015
GDP in CFA francs (billions)	1080.26	1205.08	1230.90	1344.08	1572.40	1691.42	1748.52	2404.04	2410.80	2367.41
Total budget	254.10	259.63	307.62	350.15	499.73	548.75	656.20	786.39	830.04	827.22
Total budget of the education sector	42.20	44.75	48.58	55.53	71.62	81.91	98.28	108.24	122.03	126.27
of which financed from own resources	39.79	44.75	48.58	54.53	63.85	69.48	85.01	94.20	113.06	119.95
percent of total budget that is externally financed (%)	5.7	0.0	0.0	1.8	10.8	15.2	13.5	13.0	7.3	5.0
total budget as percent of GDP (%)	3.91	3.71	3.95	4.13	4.55	4.84	5.62	4.50	5.06	5.33
total budget as percent of total spending (%)	16.61	17.24	15.79	15.86	14.33	14.93	14.98	13.76	14.70	15.26
Recurrent budget of the education sector	37.15	43.10	46.59	52.90	61.57	65.79	80.87	107.32	109.19	117.08
of which personnel	26.03	30.76	33.51	37.12	43.30	43.16	54.18	59.14	75.01	108.98
of which materials	3.65	3.66	3.95	4.25	5.21	5.04	5.31	5.37	6.70	8.10
Investment budget of the education sector	5.05	1.65	1.99	2.63	10.25	16.11	17.41	16.47	12.84	9.10
investments as percent of total spending (%)	11.97	3.69	4.10	4.74	14.31	19.67	17.71	15.22	10.52	7.21
Total budget for general education	29.58	31.53	34.62	41.69	54.11	60.64	74.74	80.48	90.90	89.27
of which primary education	14.19	18.22	18.09	23.70	34.76	41.53	45.92	50.30	56.26	56.31

(Continued)

Table 2.4 (Continued)

	2006	2007	2008	2009	2010	2011	2012	2013	2014	2015
primary education budget as percent of GDP (%)	1.31	1.51	1.47	1.76	2.21	2.46	2.63	2.09	2.33	2.38
primary education budget as percent of total spending (%)	5.58	7.02	5.88	6.77	6.96	7.57	7.00	6.40	6.78	6.81
primary education budget as percent of education sector budget (%)	33.63	40.72	37.24	42.68	48.53	50.70	46.72	46.47	46.11	44.59
of which secondary education	12.09	11.25	12.54	12.57	15.32	16.05	19.39	22.83	23.10	26.04
of which alphabetization			0.03	0.04	0.06	0.07	0.07	0.07	0.18	0.17
of which administrative budget	3.29	2.05	3.99	5.42	4.03	3.06	9.42	7.28	11.37	6.75

Source Republic of Togo, 2017

References

Bashir, Sajitha, Marlaine Lockheed, Elizabeth Ninan, and Jee-Peng Tan. 2018. *Facing Forward: Schooling for Learning in Africa*. Africa Development Forum Series. Washington, DC: World Bank. https://doi.org/10.1596/978-1-46481260-6.

Hoogeveen, Johannes, and Mariacristina Rossi. 2013. Enrollment and Grade Attainment Following the Introduction of Free Primary Education in Tanzania. *Journal of African Economies* 22 (3): 375–393.

PASEC. The Analysis Programme of the CONFEMEN Education Systems (*Programme d'Analyse des Systèmes Educatifs de la CONFEMEN*). Various Years.

Republic of Togo. Ministry of Primary and Secondary Education. National Yearbook of School Statistics (*Annuaire National des Statistiques Scolaires*). Various Years.

UNESCO, UNICEF. 2014. TOGO Rapport d'état du système éducatif. Pour une scolarisation primaire universelle et une meilleure adéquation formation-emploi. Volume 1.

The opinions expressed in this chapter are those of the author(s) and do not necessarily reflect the views of the International Bank for Reconstruction and Development/The World Bank, its Board of Directors, or the countries they represent.

Open Access This chapter is licensed under the terms of the Creative Commons Attribution 3.0 IGO License (https://creativecommons.org/licenses/by/3.0/igo/), which permits use, sharing, adaptation, distribution and reproduction in any medium or format, as long as you give appropriate credit to the International Bank for Reconstruction and Development/The World Bank, provide a link to the Creative Commons license and indicate if changes were made.

The use of the International Bank for Reconstruction and Development/The World Bank's name, and the use of the International Bank for Reconstruction and Development/The World Bank's logo, shall be subject to a separate written license agreement between the International Bank for Reconstruction and Development/The World Bank and the user and is not authorized as part of this CC-IGO license. Note that the link provided above includes additional terms and conditions of the license.

The images or other third party material in this chapter are included in the chapter's Creative Commons license, unless indicated otherwise in a credit line to the material. If material is not included in the chapter's Creative Commons license and your intended use is not permitted by statutory regulation or exceeds the permitted use, you will need to obtain permission directly from the copyright holder.

CHAPTER 3

Drivers of Performance

Johannes Hoogeveen, Mariacristina Rossi and Dario Sansone

Abstract This chapter uses the annual school census to analyze differences in primary school performances across regions. Our results, obtained from a stochastic frontier analysis, suggest that differences in efficiency explain only part of the observed variation, while resource availability is the most important driver of performance differences. In addition to this, we note that resources are distributed quite unevenly among regions and schools. By distributing more school inputs, or distributing existing inputs more equally to the benefit of underserved schools, performance can be expected to go up.

Keywords School census · Stochastic frontier analysis · Performance drivers · Regional difference · Scholastic inputs

---

J. Hoogeveen
World Bank, Washington, DC, USA
e-mail: jhoogeveen@worldbank.org

M. Rossi (✉)
School of Management and Economics, Università di Torino, Turin, Italy
e-mail: mariacristina.rossi@unito.it

D. Sansone
Georgetown University, Washington, DC, USA

© International Bank for Reconstruction
and Development/The World Bank 2019
J. Hoogeveen and M. Rossi (eds.), *Transforming Education Outcomes in Africa*, https://doi.org/10.1007/978-3-030-12708-4_3

3.1 Introduction and Motivation

As highlighted in the second chapter, Togo undeniably achieved improvements in the enrollment of primary school children. Through the combined effect of the introduction of free primary education and the absorption of community schools in the public school system, the number of students enrolled in public primary schools increased from less than 600,000 in 2006/2007 to about one million five years later. Over the same period the number of public schools increased from 3783 to 4593 and the number of classrooms from 16,538 to 23,615.

Despite the progress made, learning assessments like those done by PASEC suggest the primary education system faces important challenges in terms of education quality, with respect to regional differences in attendance (much lower in Savanes for instance) and the distribution of school inputs. This chapter aims at understanding the role school inputs play as drivers of school performance. It does so by carrying out a frontier analysis. School performance data have been drawn from administrative data on learning assessments. Specifically, we use primary school pass rates for every primary school in the country, for the 2010/2011 academic year.[1] These data are then combined with information on inputs, equally obtained for every school for the same school year. The first part of the analysis examines whether input quantities, versus inefficiency in input usage, explain differences in school outcomes. The analysis is then enriched by considering nonschool aspects, and uses *Questionnaire des Indicateurs de Base du Bien-être* (QUIBB) survey household data to assess drivers of enrollment within households.

The main contribution of this chapter is that it offers additional empirical evidence to organize the debate about resource vs. inefficiency in educational systems. Scholars have often pointed to teacher absenteeism as a main source of inefficiency and a main cause behind the dismal learning outcomes in some low- and middle-income countries. For instance, Ravallion (2016) highlighted the extremely low levels of actual teaching in India (Probe Team 1999, 2011) as well as in several other

---

[1] The analysis in this chapter focuses on the 2010/2011 school year as this is the year for which complete dataset for all schools could be obtained. Since that time investments have been made to improve the availability of school inputs, as evidenced in the previous chapter. Still as Chapter 2 demonstrates many schools and regions remain underserved, so that the assessment of this chapter remains relevant.

countries (World Bank 2004). Teacher absenteeism has also been discussed, among the others, by Kremer et al. (2005), Banerjee and Duflo (2006), Chaudhury et al. (2006), and Duflo et al. (2012). As a result, many researchers have focused their effort to analyze how to provide stronger incentives to teachers (Glewwe et al. 2010). Similarly, school and teacher autonomy have been extensively discussed in Woessmann (2003), Fuchs and Woessmann (2007), and Hanushek et al. (2013).

This chapter finds that, while it is true that inefficiencies are widespread and substantial, school resources are key determinants of educational outcomes. In other words, while it is true that reducing inefficiency may improve student performance, it is important not to forget that much basic infrastructure is simply lacking. This result is in line with the role of school inputs emphasized in Angrist and Lavy (1999), Case and Deaton (1999), and Krueger (1999). The evidence from our analysis of the school census suggests that gains brought about by increasing efficiency may be marginal compared to the huge potential benefits of additional school inputs. Students cannot learn without textbooks, blackboards and toilets.

3.2 Scholastic Inputs, Efficiency and Performance

By the 2010/2011 school year the primary cycle was in the midst of recovering from the combined shock of Togo's the economic and crisis which had lasted almost a decade and a half, the introduction of free universal education in 2008/2009 and the absorption of locally funded schools EDIL schools into the public system. Consequently, the fraction of children attending public schools has increased from 58% in 2006/2007 to 72% in 2011/2012 and total enrollment in public primary schools has gone up from around 600,000 in 2006/2007 to over 1,000,000 students in 2011/2012, an increase by 66% (Fig. 3.1).

Despite this increase in enrollment, primary school enrollment remains far from universal. According to the 2011 QUIBB, only about 82% of eligible children attend a primary school. Among children aged 6–11 who do not attend primary school, those from the poorest households are over-represented: 38% of children who do not go to school come from the poorest households, whereas only 6% come from a household in the top wealth quintile.

Another challenge facing the school system in 2010/2011 was the presence of large regional inequalities in almost every aspect and at

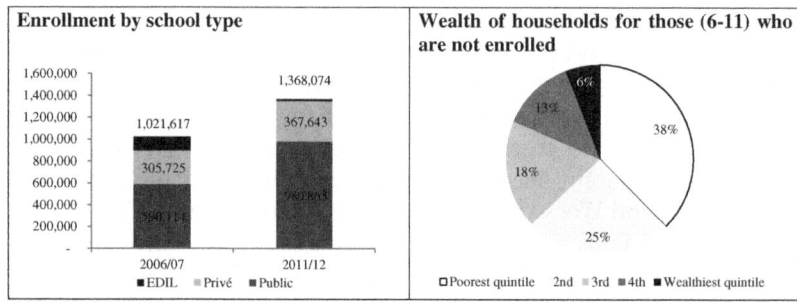

Fig. 3.1 Primary school enrollment inequalities (*Source* Authors' calculations based on the Ministry of Education 2010/2011 EMIS Data Base and QUIBB 2011)

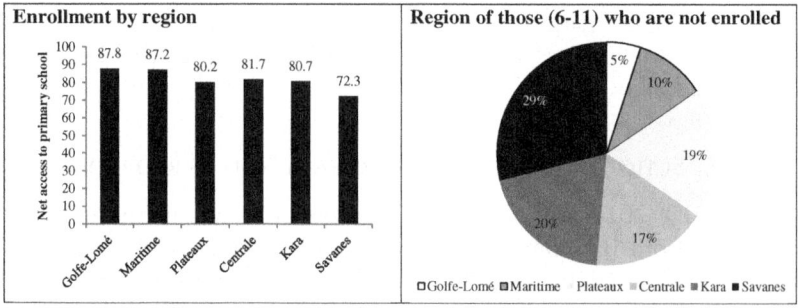

Fig. 3.2 Primary school enrollment (*Source* Authors' calculations based on QUIBB 2011)

almost every level. The further north one goes, the worse the results are. The Savanes region, in the upper north of the country is often the worst off, while the coastal regions Golfe-Lomé and Maritime are typically the best off. This gap can be illustrated with school access: the average enrollment rate in Togo is 82%, but this rate increases up to 87% in the coastal regions, whereas in Savanes it is only 72%. Almost a third of the children aged 6–11 who are not enrolled in a primary school can be found in Savanes, even though only 12% of the Togolese population resides there (Fig. 3.2).

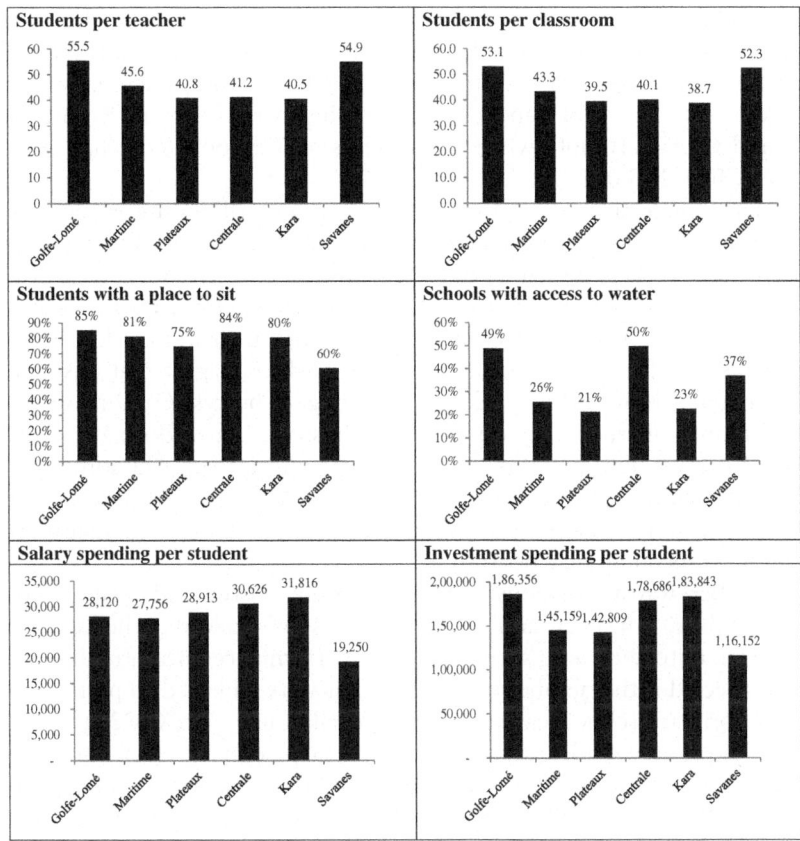

Fig. 3.3 School characteristics: 2010–2011 (*Source* Authors' calculations based on Ministry of Education 2010/2011 EMIS Data Base)

As shown in Fig. 3.3, these stark gaps are reflected in differences in scholastic inputs. The number of students per teacher varies from around 40 in Kara to over 55 in Golfe-Lomé and Savanes. In Plateaux the average number of students per classroom is 40; in Golfe-Lomé is 53. In Savanes, only 60% of students sit at a desk; in Golfe-Lomé, 85% of students do so. In Plateaux, only 21% of schools have access to water; in Golfe-Lomé and Central, about half the schools have such access. In terms of spending, the differences are equally striking. Salary spending per student (taking into account differences in payments for different type of staff) in Savanes is 60% of that in Kara. The same holds for the total amount spent on investments. Considering the total outlays for buildings, toilets, desks and chairs, spending per student in Savanes is around CFAF 116,000, while for students in Kara 60% more had been spent CFAF 183,000.

At the prefecture, or at the school level, inequalities are even more pronounced. This can be illustrated with the number of students per classroom. At the national level, the average for public schools is 43 students per class, but at the regional level this varies from 39 to 53 students per class. At the prefecture level, the range goes from as low as 16 students per class to as much as 103. It is hard to imagine that this kind of variability is an efficient way of allocating resources. Cantons where the number of students is only 16 per classroom have too many classrooms (or too few students). Cantons with more than a hundred students per classroom may have so many students in a classroom that it becomes plausible that very little learning takes place, implying that most education spending may be wasted.

Another way to demonstrate the relation between adequate scholastic inputs, efficiency and performance is by exploring the relation between outcomes and spending. The performance measure that we have selected is the number of students that were admitted to participate in the primary school leaving exam (not all students in CM2, the last grade in primary school, are allowed to participate in the exam) over the total number of students in the school. Children that pass the *Certificat d'études du premier degré* (CEPD) exam are allowed to proceed to secondary school. We prefer this measure over a more direct measure (such as the fraction of students that have passed the exam) because there is a reason to suspect that schools and students behave strategically with respect to who takes and passes the exam.

This defined, one notes the existence of large differences in our performance measure (Fig. 3.4). Some cantons like Kozah in the Kara region, and Grande Lomé (GL) do well with respectively 12 and 11% of students admitted to the final exam. Others do poorly, such as Akebou in Plateaux of Kpendjal and Oti in the Savanes regions whose performance ratios are only a third of those of the aforementioned cantons (4%). Cantons in the northern region (Savanes) do particularly poorly. Beyond the fact that Centrale and Kara do better than Plateaux, with Maritime in

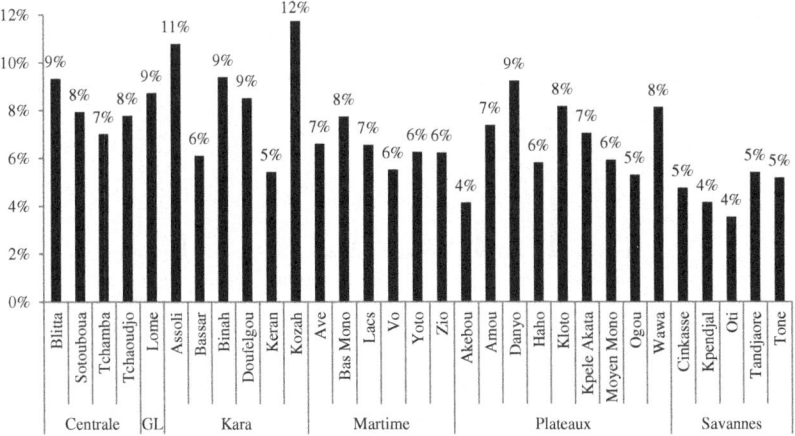

Fig. 3.4 School performance by canton in 2010/2011 (*Note* School performance is defined as the number of students that have been admitted to participating in the primary school leaving exam over the total number of students in the school. *Source* Authors' calculations based on Ministry of Education 2011/2012 EMIS Data Base)

an intermediate position, the most striking about the figure is the large degree of intra-regional variation.

On the spending side, we calculate the annual spending on teacher salaries per student, taking into account differences in grade and levels of teacher pay.[2] As spending on teachers makes up about 84% of the total primary education budget, it is a good proxy for total spending.

Figure 3.5 shows once again striking differences among regions. Indeed, if we look at payment grades for civil servants, the majority of teachers in Lomé are in grade C, while in all the other except Savanes they are mainly in grade B.

Figure 3.6 illustrates the relation between outcomes and expenditure. The graph presents for all public schools a measure of school performance (on the vertical axis) and a measure of spending (on the horizontal axis). Each dot in Fig. 3.6 represents a public school. The figure can

---

[2]Voluntary teacher receives about CFAF 90,000 per annum whereas a civil servant receives almost 2 million and an assistant teacher 1.3 million.

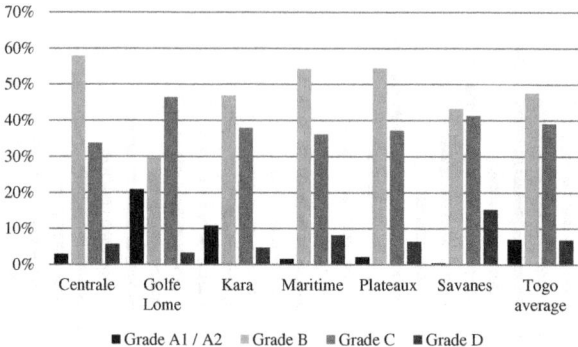

Fig. 3.5 Distribution of teachers of different grade levels by region (*Source* Government of Togo, National Yearbook of School Statistics, 2010/2011)

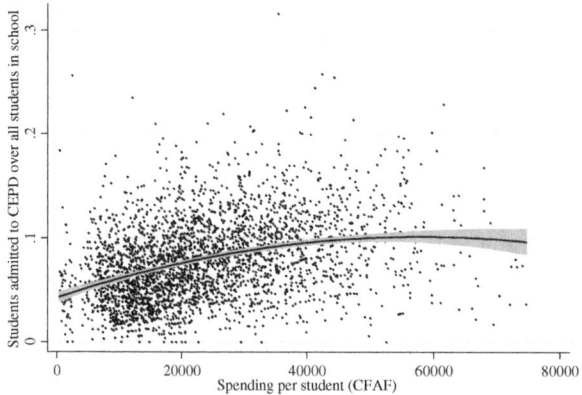

Fig. 3.6 Teacher spending per student and school performance (public schools only) (*Source* Authors' calculations)

now be used to identify those schools that do particularly well: these are the schools with the best performance for a given level of spending.

The line in Fig. 3.6 presents local averages. This line is upward sloping suggesting that more inputs (or more spending per student) lead to better results. This plot emphasizes that certain schools perform poorly given the resources they receive (those below the line do worse than average), while others (those above the line) do better than average. Excellent are those schools that lie furthest above the regression line.

This figure can also be used to demonstrate, despite not making any causality claims, that within the universe of schools in Togo there is scope for efficiency improvements through efficiency gains. Some schools receiving CFAF 20,000 per student do extremely poorly and have a performance ratio of around zero, whereas others have performance ratios higher than 0.1. By bringing the schools up to at least the average (of about 0.9) significant advances can be made without incurring additional spending.

The discussion so far has only illustrated that both inputs and efficiency matter for performance. Which of these factors matter most, and which inputs are more important, cannot be inferred from these descriptive statistics. To deepen our study, we need to turn to regression analysis, which is presented in the remainder of the chapter.

3.3 Data

The main datasets used in the regression analysis are Primary School Census data, particularly those for the 2010/2011 academic year. This dataset comprises detailed information for each school for a total of 6158 observations. Table 3.1 shows the distribution of the schools across regions: the relative majority (around 25%) is located in the Plateaux region, while the region with the smallest number of schools is Savanes. Our analysis is centered on the ratio of admitted students to the final exam of primary school (CEPD) over the total number of students in

Table 3.1 Number of schools by region

	Initial data		Sample data	
	Freq.	Percent	Freq.	Percent
Centrale	761	12.36	492	11.26
Golfe-Lomé	992	16.11	672	15.38
Kara	882	14.32	699	16.00
Maritime	1187	19.28	820	18.77
Plateaux	1595	25.90	1143	26.17
Savanes	741	12.03	542	12.41
Total	6158	100	4368	100

Source Ministry of Education 2010/2011 EMIS Data Base

the school. To construct this variable, we merged the 2010/2011 and 2011/2012 school census data, since in the 2010/2011 census information about admissions to the exam was not present. Indeed, the exam results are reported in the school census the following year.

The school census data sets only present school information, but in our regression we also want to include nonschool variables as controls, such as the level of education of the population living in proximity of the school in a region. Such information is available from the poverty map that was constructed by combining the population census (*Quatrième Recensement Général de la Population et de l'Habitat*, RGPH4) of 2009 and the household survey QUIBB of 2011. It was not possible to match school level information to census or poverty map information, but at the canton level this was possible. But even then, it was not always possible to obtain a correct match and some observations were lost in this process. For instance, some schools were dropped because the total number of students admitted to CEPD was bigger than the total number of students in CM2. As a result, the number of observations used in the estimations is reduced to 4368. The last two columns of Table 3.1 display the final data, which are used in the analysis.

An overview of the main variables used in the regression can be found in the Appendix. Here we consider some of them, which are correlated to our main variable of interest: the percent of students admitted to the CEPD over the total number of students in the school. Figure 3.7

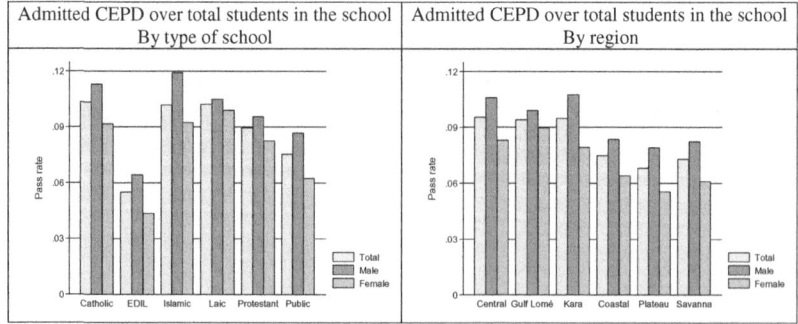

Fig. 3.7 Performance by school type and by region (*Note* Schools whose pass rate was equal to 0 have been dropped. *Source* Authors' calculations based on Ministry of Education 2010/2011 and 2011/2012 EMIS Data Base)

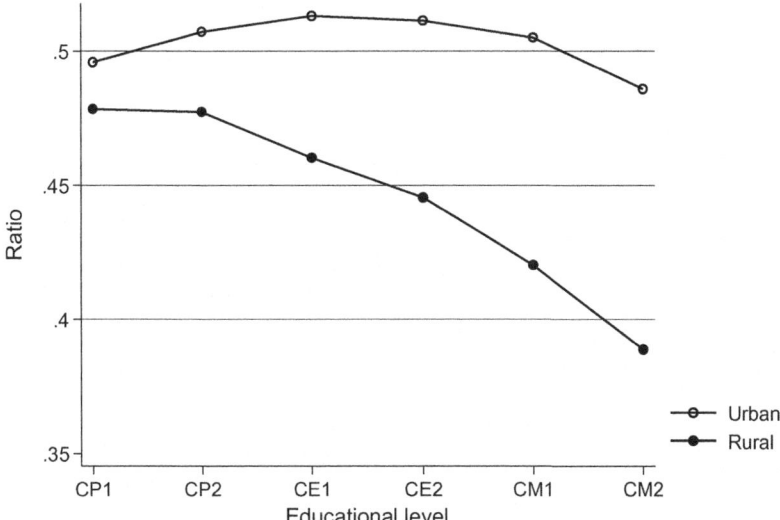

Fig. 3.8 Ratio of female over male students by grade in rural and urban areas (*Note* Male students are the complement to one of female student. *Source* Authors' calculations based on Ministry of Education 2010/2011 and 2011/2012 EMIS Data Base)

shows how schools performed on average by school type (Public, EDIL, Catholic, Islamic, Protestant and Laic) and by region. The figure shows that the best performing schools are private schools and that Kara, Lomé and Centrale are the regions with the highest levels of performance. It is also interesting to note the gender dimension of school performances, which suggests that in all regions and across all school types boys perform better than girls: this in contrast to what is generally found in non-developing countries. The difference in performance is least pronounced in Laic schools and in Lomé, and most pronounced in Community and Islamic schools.

Figure 3.8 provides further information about the gender issue: the ratio between girls in CP1, the first year of primary school and total number of students in CP1 does not differ substantially between urban and rural areas. Nevertheless, while this ratio remains roughly stable for higher educational levels in cities, there is a steady decline of female students across classes in the countryside. Indeed, in CP1 the ratio is 47.9%

(49.6% in urban areas), whereas in the last year of primary school CM2 is 38.9% (48.6% in urban areas).

3.4 Estimation Results

Table 3.2 contains the main regression result using a stochastic frontier technique.[3]

We first present our basic specification (column 1) and a richer specification in column (2). It is worth mentioning that the dependent variable is the ratio—not the percentage—of students admitted to the CEPD over the total number of students in the school. This explains why, at first sight, the coefficients in Table 3.2 have small magnitude.

Although the main aim of this chapter is to measure school inefficiency, i.e. to analyze the residuals from the frontier analysis, it is interesting to look at some of the regressors. However, it should be stressed that we cannot attach a causal interpretation to such coefficients. One of the main results is that private school show better results. This is in line with Pereira and Moreira (2007). Nevertheless, private schools are likely to be more expensive, so we should not infer from this that private schools use their resources in a more efficient way. In fact, if private schools paid their teachers better, one would expect these schools to perform better. In the absence of information on the actual cost of schools, the best we can do is to just illustrate by using a dummy variable the differences between private and public schools and note that a cost-benefit analysis would be a very useful contribution of future work. It is also worth noting that the regressions are not able to control neither for family background nor for knowledge of children at school start (i.e. kindergarten attendance). Hence, the magnitude of the private school variable

---

[3] The frontier technique is defined as follows: $y_i = f(x_i, \beta) + v_i - u_i$, here, y_i is the output of school i, our measure of performance, $f(.)$ is a measurable production function, x_i are exogenous variables, β is a vector of unknown parameters and $v_i - u_i$ is the composed error term consisting of v, the symmetric disturbance (idiosyncratic effect), and u, the non-negative disturbance measuring the inefficiency of the school (productive inefficiency). The random errors v_i are usually assumed to be independently and identically distributed $N(0; \sigma_v^2)$, and independent from the u_i. The most common assumption for the inefficiency term is the half-normal distribution (Aigner et al. 1977), i.e. the non-negative truncation of the $N(0; \sigma_u^2)$. We use the Stata command *frontier* to perform the analysis, with the default half normal distribution in the model. We also performed the analysis by using a Tobit analysis and we also excluded thee top 255. However, the results have not changed substantially.

Table 3.2 Frontier analysis for ratio of admitted CEPD students over total students in school

	(1)	(2)
Private school (d)	0.014015***	0.021946***
	(0.0013)	(0.0044)
Number of teachers in the school	−0.001223**	−0.000426
	(0.0004)	(0.0004)
Teachers-students ratio	0.002554***	0.001466**
	(0.0005)	(0.0005)
Female ratio in CM2	0.026710***	0.022680***
	(0.0034)	(0.0033)
Average student age in CM2	−0.001066*	−0.000656
	(0.0005)	(0.0005)
CP1–CP2 taught together (d)	0.005535***	0.004637**
	(0.0016)	(0.0015)
CE1–CE2 taught together	−0.001050	0.000501
	(0.0016)	(0.0015)
CM1–CM2 taught together (d)	−0.027240***	−0.022625***
	(0.0014)	(0.0014)
Employment ratio	−0.000615***	−0.000162*
	(0.0001)	(0.0001)
Net enrollment rate—primary	0.000054	0.000358***
	(0.0001)	(0.0001)
Urban (d)	0.006201***	0.007130***
	(0.0013)	(0.0014)
Average qualification teachers in private school		−0.004470*
		(0.0018)
Ratio of permanent teachers		−0.008761***
		(0.0021)
Repeating students rate		−0.056092***
		(0.0044)
Ln Average teacher age		0.016199***
		(0.0042)
Gender Headmaster (d)		0.008066***
		(0.0018)
Average qualification teachers		0.002982**
		(0.0009)
Seats every 100 students		−0.000041
		(0.0000)
Desks every 100 students		0.000284***
		(0.0000)
Toilets every 100 student		0.001490***
		(0.0004)

(continued)

Table 3.2 (continued)

	(1)	(2)
Water in school		−0.000092
		(0.0011)
Math books per students		0.003174
		(0.0023)
Reading books per students		0.002538
		(0.0018)
Dependency ratio		0.001847***
		(0.0001)
Enrollment rate (secondary school)		0.000363***
		(0.0001)
Constant	0.127766***	−0.112837***
lnsig2v	−6.889271***	−7.068340***
	(0.0214)	(0.0225)
lnsig2u	−16.88815	−17.02233
	(108.2370)	(63.9037)
Lambda	.006748	.006908
Observations	4368	3957

Standard errors in parentheses
*$p<0.05$, **$p<0.01$, ***$p<0.001$

is likely to be affected by endogeneity issues, as it is likely that students from high socio-economic status self-select into private schools.

The results show that additional teachers are associated with increasing performance. On average, the pass rate is between 0.14 and 0.25 percentage points higher in schools with an additional teacher per every hundred students.

We now turn to the gender composition of the class. Given the high drop-out rate of females, we expect that a higher female to male ratio could lead to an average improvement, if the girls in school are a selected sample and are better than average students. The coefficient of female students over total students in CM2 is positive and strongly significant, thus implying also a substantial peer effect: the more numerous are the girls with respect to boys in the class, the higher is the school performance.

Older students in class do have a detrimental effect on the overall performance, but this effect holds in the most parsimonious specification only. Similarly, schools regularly merge classes, so it is important to see the effect of such a policy. Unexpectedly, if the first two years (CP1–CP2) are taught together, the effect is positive and significant. This result might signal an imitation effect that at young age, it could be beneficial for all children (in a similar vein with kindergarten). Conversely, the effect is strongly negative and significant for the last two grades (CM1–CM2), thus suggesting that classes with more than one advanced course taught simultaneously might have detrimental effects on learning. This result is very robust and corroborates the hypothesis that the learning environment is something policy-makers should focus on. Indeed, the magnitude of the last coefficient is rather high: teaching CM1–CM2 together are associated with a reduction of more than 2 percentage points in the outcome.

Employment rate in the canton in which the school is located acts as detrimental to performance, possibly because it acts as a proxy for the fact that parents have fewer opportunities to spend time with their children after school. From a geographical point of view, urban schools perform better than rural ones on average.

In the richer specification, we include additional variables, which could impact the outcome of interest. Considering the qualification of teachers, the effect is strongly significant and positive. Qualification of teachers in private schools, in contrast, gives approximately no impact, if anything. The ratio of repeating students is negatively related with the pass rate, as expected. Teacher experience (approximated by age) has a strong correlation with school performance. Furthermore, if the school headmaster is a woman, resources seem to be used more efficiently: ceteris paribus, a female headmaster is associated with an increase of around one percentage point in the pass rate.

We also add among the regressors the ratio of permanent teachers out of total teachers. One might expect that the number of permanent teachers could positively affect the overall performance. Indeed, through a selection effect, the permanent teachers should be more likely to be better teachers within an efficient recruitment system. However, the results work towards an opposite direction: the higher the ratio of permanent teachers, the lower is the school performance. We thus infer that increasing teacher quality is not correlated with hiring more permanent teachers.

In addition to this, the characteristics of the school premises do matter: desk number significantly affects the frontier as the quality of infrastructure shows an important role. The more desks are available, the higher the performance. The availability of desks has an enormous importance and, remarkably, toilets as well. An additional toilet for every hundred students has the same impact of an additional teacher. Possibly, this result could reflect better hygienic conditions, which, in turn, would turn into better health and higher performance.

We now turn our attention to the most important element of this analysis. The estimate of λ is reported at the end of Table 3.2. This parameter is defined as

$$\lambda = \frac{\sigma_u}{\sigma_v}$$

and it is not statistically different from zero. When λ goes close to $+\infty$, then all variation from the frontier is due to the inefficiency term, then it should be better to use the deterministic approach to estimate such frontier. On the other hand, if λ is close to 0—as in our case—a stochastic frontier is a more appropriate choice.

A critical result of our analysis is the low variability in the inefficiency term u_i. This implies that it is possible to distinguish between more and less efficient schools, but the key factor explaining differences in performance is the presence of inputs (and the noise component of the error term). In other words, differences in the pass rate are due mainly to lack of resources rather than technical inefficiency. We want to stress this result as it is crucial for the policy standpoint. Resources are distributed unevenly among regions and schools, and their distribution is the main driver of differences in results.

In Table 3.3, we present predicted performance by quintile of performance and the region in which the school is located. The schools requiring most attention i.e. the worst performing schools, are concentrated in Plateaux and Savanes, while few poorly performing schools are found in

Table 3.3 Predicted school performance, by quintile and region

Quintile	Centrale	Lomé	Kara	Maritime	Plateaux	Savanes	Total
Worst performing	4.7	0.3	12.5	17.8	42.5	22.3	100
2	9.1	9.8	16.3	16.2	30.5	18.1	100
3	11.1	17.3	13.0	21.0	27.3	10.1	100
4	16.6	22.7	14.1	15.16	22.2	9.5	100
Best performing	15.7	24.4	31.0	8.0	14.1	6.8	100
Total	11.4	14.9	17.4	15.6	27.3	13.4	100

Lomé and Centrale. The second best performers show a percentage of 10% in Savanes and the highest in Golfe-Lomé and Plateaux. Targeting poorest performing school does not mean targeting a region in particular, at least with the exception of Golfe-Lomé, where the percentage of worst performing school is negligible.

One possible concern with our empirical strategy is that individuals may move in order to gain access to a better school. First of all, it should be noted that Togo is a low-income country, thus there are high information asymmetries and parents may not know enough to judge the quality of a school. Second, in order to address this potential issue, we have looked at the data available from MICS 2010, a representative survey of the population in Togo. If parents did send their children to other family members in order to give them the opportunity to attend high-quality schools, we would observe these movements in the household composition. However, if we consider only household members aged between 5 and 12 who attended school in the academic year 2010/2011, the vast majority (almost 80%) was the household head's child. Furthermore, once we exclude orphans and children whose parents lived in the same households even if they were not the household head, we are left with 10% of children, which may have moved to a different household because of school quality. Nevertheless, this is a (relatively small) upper bound since parents may also send their children to their relatives because they have to work or they do not have the money to feed and raise them. It is thus plausible that economic reasons were pivotal among poorer households. Keeping this into account, only 3.6% of all the children in the relevant age group attending school were sent to relatives who belonged to the top two wealth quintiles.

A similar kind of student selection may occur if the whole household moved to a neighborhood with higher-quality school. Although this is usual in developed countries such as the United States, it seems unlikely in this context given the tight budget constraint. Indeed, as discussed in IMF (2014), migration in Togo is mainly driven by economic rather than educational opportunities. Thus, given the above discussion, we can conclude that sample selection due to student mobility was extremely limited and should not affect the validity of our results.

3.5 The Demand Side: Determinants of School Enrollment

This section focuses on the demand side: we look at the drivers behind a child enrollment status and examine it as a household decision. We do so by making use of QUIBB for the determinants of school enrollment and achievements. More in detail, as for the determinants of the school demand, we have mainly relied on the two waves of QUIBB, i.e. 2006 and 2011. This survey contains 7500 households who were interviewed in Togo during the first wave, including 36,430 individuals, whereas 5532 households and 29,781 individuals took part in the second wave. This repeated cross-section is extremely useful for the purpose of our research since it provides several information on household composition, education3, health, employment, assets, current expenditure, auto-consumption and income.

Table 3.4 shows the results about the determinants of school enrollment. The dependent variable is a dummy which is equal to 1 if the respondent was attending school at the time of the interview. Therefore, since this enrollment decision is represented by an indicator variable, it has been necessary to use a binary choice model, i.e. a Probit model. Only individuals aged between 6 and 15 years have been considered. The main dataset used in this analysis has been QUIBB 2006 and 2011, thus it has been possible to examine two time periods.

Column 1 in Table 3.4 contains a basic specification (17,968 observations), while Columns 2 and 3 show an extended model computed used Probit and Logit estimation methods respectively. Furthermore, in the last two columns the sample have been splitted: the same probit regression of Column 2 has been run for individuals aged 6–8 (Column 5) and 9–15 (Column 6). Marginal effects instead of coefficients are shown in all models displayed in Table 3.4.

First of all, it is interesting to note how household composition affects the variable of interest: if there are small children (aged 0–4), the respondents are less likely to go to school, especially for older individuals (age 9–15, Column 6). This is probably due to the fact that older children are expected to take care of their younger siblings while their parents work. In a specular way, a higher number of adults in the household increases the probability of going to school: this effect is statistically significant for individuals aged 9–15, but not for those aged 6–8.

3 DRIVERS OF PERFORMANCE

Table 3.4 Enrollment probability (6–15). Probit and Logit

	(1)	(2)	(3)	(4)	(5)	(6)
	Probit	Probit	Logit	Parents	Age 6–8	Age 9–15
Number babies (0–4)	−0.009536**	−0.015749***	−0.014215***	−0.010078**	−0.003768	−0.013079***
	(0.0029)	(0.0029)	(0.0027)	(0.0032)	(0.0053)	(0.0034)
Number children (5–15)	0.002937	−0.001219	−0.001553	−0.001513	0.004260	−0.005575**
	(0.0018)	(0.0018)	(0.0016)	(0.0020)	(0.0033)	(0.0020)
Number adults (>15)	0.010926***	0.006534***	0.006505***	0.007948***	0.006054	0.004103*
	(0.0019)	(0.0019)	(0.0018)	(0.0022)	(0.0038)	(0.0020)
Household head female (d)		0.087154***	0.077686***	0.051411	0.103630***	0.074406***
		(0.0089)	(0.0082)	(0.0295)	(0.0182)	(0.0095)
Max education household (head vs. spouse)	0.019071***	0.017899***	0.017219***		0.023082***	0.015509***
	(0.0008)	(0.0008)	(0.0008)		(0.0015)	(0.0009)
Education father				0.015220***		
				(0.0011)		
Education mother				0.016733***		
				(0.0017)		
Mother alive (d)	0.038971***	0.038243***	0.034367***	0.010327	0.019186	0.050210***
	(0.0106)	(0.0106)	(0.0100)	(0.0167)	(0.0209)	(0.0121)
Father alive (d)	−0.042709***	0.044743***	0.039024**	0.100819	−0.004914	0.069396***
	(0.0094)	(0.0150)	(0.0144)	(0.0832)	(0.0277)	(0.0173)

(continued)

Table 3.4 (continued)

	(1) Probit	(2) Probit	(3) Logit	(4) Parents	(5) Age 6–8	(6) Age 9–15
Self-production (d)	−0.067156***	−0.034760***	−0.035749***	−0.046613***	−0.084934***	−0.010314
	(0.0092)	(0.0100)	(0.0097)	(0.0133)	(0.0187)	(0.0115)
Ln (total private expenditure pc)	0.010683*	0.003855	0.004912	−0.000568	0.016955	−0.006555
	(0.0052)	(0.0072)	(0.0068)	(0.0085)	(0.0134)	(0.0082)
Interaction female expenditure pc		−0.021715*	−0.021228*	−0.000416	−0.001820	−0.027496**
		(0.0090)	(0.0084)	(0.0110)	(0.0171)	(0.0103)
Female (d)	−0.077767***	0.121829	0.122475	−0.061594	−0.036690	0.166837
	(0.0059)	(0.0826)	(0.0785)	(0.1028)	(0.1577)	(0.0936)
Neither son nor daughter (d)	−0.040536**	−0.008533	−0.007583		0.001317	−0.001968
	(0.0135)	(0.0137)	(0.0129)		(0.0265)	(0.0150)
Distance from primary school (time)	−0.023282***	−0.022869***	−0.021251***	−0.021924***	−0.037859***	−0.012966***
	(0.0030)	(0.0030)	(0.0027)	(0.0033)	(0.0055)	(0.0035)
Distance from secondary school (time)	−0.018785***	−0.013494***	−0.012893***	−0.014691***	−0.014760**	−0.013181***
	(0.0027)	(0.0027)	(0.0025)	(0.0031)	(0.0050)	(0.0031)

(continued)

Table 3.4 (continued)

	(1)	(2)	(3)	(4)	(5)	(6)
	Probit	Probit	Logit	Parents	Age 6–8	Age 9–15
Distance from health center (time)	−0.012749***	−0.009116***	−0.008110***	−0.008281**	−0.008028	−0.009386**
	(0.0027)	(0.0027)	(0.0025)	(0.0031)	(0.0050)	(0.0030)
Distance from food market (time)	0.010540***	0.010266***	0.009417***	0.013211***	0.012075*	0.008858**
	(0.0027)	(0.0027)	(0.0025)	(0.0031)	(0.0048)	(0.0031)
Distance from public transport (time)	−0.003249	−0.013391***	−0.012321***	−0.013644***	−0.016654***	−0.011033***
	(0.0025)	(0.0025)	(0.0023)	(0.0028)	(0.0047)	(0.0029)
Household owns a mobile phone (d)		0.030277***	0.028124***	0.041016***	0.025310	0.035050***
		(0.0081)	(0.0077)	(0.0095)	(0.0156)	(0.0089)
Wave 2—2011 (d)		0.096733***	0.091663***	0.084659***	0.134950***	0.073701***
		(0.0070)	(0.0066)	(0.0080)	(0.0131)	(0.0080)
Maritime (d)	0.065625***	0.030963*	0.032443*	−0.016715	−0.110058**	0.064731***
	(0.0130)	(0.0141)	(0.0139)	(0.0248)	(0.0410)	(0.0127)
Plateaux (d)	0.016873	−0.024030	−0.023167	−0.077117**	−0.114090**	−0.004855
	(0.0153)	(0.0164)	(0.0168)	(0.0282)	(0.0418)	(0.0167)
Centrale (d)	0.073699***	0.041266**	0.040363**	−0.003310	−0.053425	0.060319***
	(0.0133)	(0.0143)	(0.0139)	(0.0250)	(0.0412)	(0.0133)

(continued)

Table 3.4 (continued)

	(1)	(2)	(3)	(4)	(5)	(6)
	Probit	Probit	Logit	Parents	Age 6-8	Age 9-15
Kara (d)	0.015299	−0.016422	−0.015410	−0.064770*	−0.118776**	0.007893
	(0.0156)	(0.0169)	(0.0171)	(0.0287)	(0.0446)	(0.0166)
Savanes (d)	−0.051193**	−0.080123***	−0.071915***	−0.098382***	−0.165483***	−0.064928**
	(0.0177)	(0.0188)	(0.0194)	(0.0289)	(0.0444)	(0.0201)
Observations	17,968	16,797	16,797	11,647	5893	10,904
Pseudo R-squared	0.125	0.145	0.146	0.177	0.175	0.146
Log_likelihood	−8087.87	−7136.91	−7129.15	−4870.15	−2721.85	−4252.39

Marginal effects. Robust standard errors in parentheses. Lomé is taken as reference region Individuals aged 6-15 are asked if they currently go to school. Education level is in years of school. Distances are reported as 15 min intervals. (d) for discrete change of dummy variable from 0 to 1. The following variables have not reported because not significant: dummy whether the household worked in the last 7 days, distance from water source (time), interaction female dummy with household auto-consumes, interaction female dummy with distance from water source (time), interaction female dummy with number of baby aged 0-2 in the household, ln(OECD equivalent private expenditure per capita), the household own a computer (d)
*p<0.05, **p<0.01, ***p<0.001

The maximum education level of the household head (or of the spouse if higher) have a positive and significant effect in all specifications. In line with this finding, Column 4 shows the effects of mother's and father's education[4] on their offsprings'[5]: both variables have a positive and significant effect, and mother's education has a bigger impact than father's. Another relevant variable is the distance from primary school[6]: the effect is negative and strongly significant in all specifications.

If the household head is a woman, children are more likely to go to school (Column 2). The coefficient is statistically significant. Moreover, if parents are alive and live in the same household, the enrollment probability increases for individuals aged 6–15 and 9–15—and the effect is bigger for the mother rather than the father—whereas it is not significant for respondent aged 6–8. In addition to this, children who live in households producing part of the goods consumed by the members themselves are less likely to attend school, especially if aged between 6 and 8, probably because they are involved in the production process.

Quite surprisingly, neither the natural logarithm of total consumption per capita nor the gender indicator has some significant effect. On the other hand, the interaction between these two variables is negative and significant (albeit it is no longer significant when only people aged 6–8 are considered). The actual and potential impact of ICT on the education process is stressed by the positive and significant effect of mobile phones: the dummy signaling whether the household owns a mobile phone has a positive and significant coefficient both for children aged 6–15 and 9–15.

In line with the descriptive statistics, the improvements observed between 2006 and 2011 are reflected in the positive and significant coefficient of the time dummy. Finally, from a geographical point of view, Savanna seems the region where children are less likely to go to school, whereas Coastal Region have a positive and significant coefficient in

---

[4] Therefore, the variable "Max education in the household (head vs. spouse)" have been dropped.

[5] Since only natural sons and daughters have been included in this regression, the variable "No son nor daughter" have been omitted.

[6] Distances are reported as 15 min intervals. In other words, the variable distance from primary school takes value 1 if the respondent spent up to 14 minutes to go to school, 2 if the time was between 15 and 29 minutes, 3 between 30 and 44, 4 between 45 and 60, 5 if the student had to travel more than an hour to reach her primary school.

Column 2 (age 6–15), as well as in Column 6 (age 9–15), whereas the estimated relation is negative and significant in Column 5 (age 6–8). Central Region has a positive and significant coefficient both in Columns 2 and 6 (Lomé has been taken as a reference point in order to avoid perfect multicollinearity).

In the first two columns of Table 3.5, the same model as in Table 3.4 (Column 2) has been estimated while distinguishing between waves. The remarkable improvements achieved during that period are highlighted by the weaker coefficients of the regional dummies in 2011 than 2006. Indeed, only the marginal effect of Coastal remained still significant in wave 2, thus regional differences had almost disappeared between 2006 and 2011. Moreover, the self-production dummy—which is equal to 1 if the household produced (part of) the goods which consumed—was no longer significant in 2011: this may be interpreted as a good signal since more children enrolled in school in 2011 instead of working within the household.

The last column of Table 3.5 includes the natural logarithm of public expenditure on primary school per student and the total number of students in primary schools in 2011. In this specification it was not possible to include all regional dummies, otherwise there would have been perfect collinearity. Therefore, only two dummies for Gulf Lomé and Savanna have been added. Contrary to what was expected, the coefficient of public expenditure is significant and negative.

In order to deepen our analysis, we have considered not only whether individuals were attending school at the time of the interview, but also the highest educational level achieved by individuals between age 6 and 15. To do so, Table 3.6 takes as dependent variable the respondent's years of education. In order to avoid a selection bias, we have used the Heckman estimation method: the selection variable is a dummy which indicates whether the individual had ever been to school. As reported at the end of the table, the arthrho is statistically different from 0, therefore taking into account such selection bias seems the appropriate procedure.

Similarly to the findings of the probit analysis, if there are babies in the households aged 0–4 years, there is a negative and significant effect on educational achievements, while the number of adults, as well as the number of children (which was not significant previously), have positive and significant coefficients. Affiliation matters: not being the household head's child does not affect the probability of attending school, as shown

Table 3.5 Enrollment probability (6–15)

	(1)	(2)	(3)
	Wave 1 2006	Wave 2 2011	Wave 2 2011
Ln (public expenditure per student)			−0.021263*
			(0.0104)
Number babies (0–4)	−0.017364***	−0.013502***	−0.013567***
	(0.0052)	(0.0032)	(0.0032)
Number children (5–15)	0.004497	−0.003336	−0.003596
	(0.0032)	(0.0019)	(0.0019)
Number adults (>15)	0.006718*	0.007983***	0.008550***
	(0.0033)	(0.0022)	(0.0021)
Household head female (d)	0.089179***	0.079338***	0.079188***
	(0.0150)	(0.0101)	(0.0101)
Max Education household (head vs. spouse)	0.020015***	0.014812***	0.014700***
	(0.0012)	(0.0010)	(0.0010)
Mother alive (d)	0.060079***	0.022886	0.022338
	(0.0170)	(0.0127)	(0.0126)
Father alive (d)	0.042476	0.046604*	0.046728*
	(0.0236)	(0.0181)	(0.0182)
Self-production (d)	−0.069504***	−0.007687	−0.008930
	(0.0154)	(0.0129)	(0.0128)
Ln (Total private expenditure per capita)	0.019910	0.001414	0.003484
	(0.0123)	(0.0086)	(0.0087)
Interaction female expenditure pc	−0.023518	−0.017503	−0.018331
	(0.0147)	(0.0106)	(0.0107)
Female (d)	0.126068	0.095617	0.103128
	(0.1336)	(0.0988)	(0.0995)
Neither son nor daughter (d)	−0.009036	−0.004765	−0.004654
	(0.0224)	(0.0160)	(0.0160)
Distance from primary school (time)	−0.021042***	−0.021572***	−0.021070***
	(0.0050)	(0.0035)	(0.0035)
Distance from secondary school (time)	−0.011658**	−0.013822***	−0.014354***
	(0.0042)	(0.0034)	(0.0034)
Distance from health center (time)	−0.010664*	−0.007527*	−0.007297*
	(0.0043)	(0.0032)	(0.0032)
Distance from food market (time)	0.009067*	0.007603*	0.005984
	(0.0039)	(0.0036)	(0.0036)
Distance from public transport (time)	−0.018609***	−0.006433	−0.005588
	(0.0038)	(0.0034)	(0.0034)
Household owns a mobile phone (d)	0.046768**	0.026563**	0.028335**
	(0.0159)	(0.0089)	(0.0089)
Savanes (d)	−0.101121***	−0.018133	−0.055660***

(continued)

Table 3.5 (continued)

	(1)	(2)	(3)
	Wave 1 2006	Wave 2 2011	Wave 2 2011
Lomé (d)	(0.0273)	(0.0239)	(0.0120) −0.017324 (0.0251)
Maritime (d)	0.063014** (0.0204)	0.045119* (0.0177)	
Plateaux (d)	−0.008878 (0.0233)	0.006479 (0.0218)	
Centrale (d)	0.077594*** (0.0201)	0.037633 (0.0193)	
Kara (d)	−0.012059 (0.0246)	0.019745 (0.0208)	
Observations	8782	8015	8015
Pseudo R-squared	0.147	0.126	0.125
Log likelihood	−4110.46	−2999.21	−3003.69

Marginal effects. Robust standard errors in parentheses. Data on public expenditure available only in 2011. (d) for discrete change of dummy variable from 0 to 1. Public expenditure includes expenditure on staff for preschool and primary education. Individuals aged 6–15 are asked if they currently go to school. Education level is in years of school. Distances are reported as 15 min intervals
*$p<0.05$, **$p<0.01$, ***$p<0.001$

in the enrollment rates estimations, but it does negatively influence the investment in more advanced education.

Again, if the head of the household is female, or she has a high level of education, children are more likely to achieve higher educational levels. Furthermore, if there is some form of self-production, or if the primary school is distant, the expected education acquired by children is lower. On the other hand, the improvements occurred over the last years are verified by the positive coefficient of the time dummy, while it should be stressed that regional differences are even higher in this model since all geographical dummies except Central have a negative and significant coefficient. Finally, in this case not only private expenditure per capita and the gender dummy are statistically insignificant, but even the interaction between these two variables is no longer significant.

Table 3.6 School achievements (6–15). Heckman

	(1)	(2)
	Year education	*Ever gone to school*
Number babies (0–4)	−0.319757***	−0.114584***
	(0.0207)	(0.0095)
Number children (5–15)	0.045969***	0.011212*
	(0.0125)	(0.0056)
Number adults (>15)	0.155505***	0.058240***
	(0.0123)	(0.0059)
Household head female (d)	0.508948***	0.197370***
	(0.0790)	(0.0380)
Max education household (head vs. spouse)	0.120820***	0.058441***
	(0.0052)	(0.0027)
Mother alive (d)	−0.184388**	−0.045599
	(0.0681)	(0.0326)
Father alive (d)	−0.391237***	−0.158442***
	(0.0917)	(0.0443)
Self-production (d)	−0.352352***	−0.188359***
	(0.0644)	(0.0351)
Ln (total private expenditure per capita)	0.042751	0.047041*
	(0.0473)	(0.0226)
Interaction female expenditure pc	0.049929	0.013097
	(0.0609)	(0.0290)
Female (d)	−1.002680	−0.367056
	(0.5717)	(0.2700)
Neither son nor daughter (d)	−0.843895***	−0.323552***
	(0.0910)	(0.0433)
Distance from primary school (time)	−0.096577***	−0.053916***
	(0.0235)	(0.0103)
Distance from secondary school (time)	−0.155219***	−0.059414***
	(0.0191)	(0.0089)
Distance from health center (time)	−0.033446	−0.025955**
	(0.0188)	(0.0088)
Distance from food market (time)	0.070442***	0.033122***
	(0.0184)	(0.0086)
Distance from public transport (time)	−0.093921***	−0.044452***
	(0.0183)	(0.0083)
Household owns a mobile phone (d)	0.264920***	0.112153***
	(0.0550)	(0.0272)
Wave 2—2011 (d)	0.475004***	0.223110***
	(0.0495)	(0.0233)
Maritime (d)	−0.245455**	−0.123515*
	(0.0856)	(0.0509)
Plateaux (d)	−0.266192**	−0.161414**

(continued)

Table 3.6 (continued)

	(1)	(2)
	Year education	Ever gone to school
Centrale (d)	(0.0926)	(0.0530)
	0.004187	−0.009589
Kara (d)	(0.0947)	(0.0545)
	−0.326618***	−0.189849***
Savanes (d)	(0.0966)	(0.0545)
	−0.696105***	−0.332999***
Constant	(0.0978)	(0.0545)
	3.527651***	1.049962***
Athrho	(0.4816)	(0.2307)
	2.845714***	
Ln(sigma)	(0.0366)	
	0.920123***	
Observations	(0.0062)	
	16,804	
Log likelihood	−3.6e+04	

Standard errors in parentheses. Lomé is taken as reference region. Individuals aged 6–15 are asked if they have ever been to school and their highest educational level. Education level is in years of school. Distances are reported as 15 min intervals
*$p<0.05$, **$p<0.01$, ***$p<0.001$

3.6 Conclusions

By 2010/2011 the public education system had made substantial improvements in enrollment. In fact, the percentage of children who had never gone to school has decreased sharply between 2006 and 2011 in all regions and across all wealth quintiles. Nevertheless, there remain significant challenges in how to bring the remaining children into school, how to accommodate the large influx of new students, how to improve levels of learning and how to reduce regional inequalities.

The assessment of the decision drivers to send one's children to school demonstrates that this decision is explained by a combination of household-specific variables and variables that can be affected through public policy. We find no evidence for the level of household expenditure mattering for school attendance and grade achievement, which is encouraging. Certain determinants fall largely outside the scope of public policy-making: household composition, or having a female household head. Other determinants can only be slowly affected by public policy, such as the level of education of one's parents. Yet other variables suggest that public resource availability matters. Distance to school, for instance, is a significant driver of the decision to attend school.

By carrying out a stochastic frontier analysis, this chapter also looked into the school-level drivers of performance (defined by passing the CEPD exam) for those students who attend school. A key result is that differences in performance between schools are mainly attributable to a lack of resources and less to differences in technical efficiency. This is an important point, because this chapter has also noted that resources are distributed unevenly among regions and schools. By improving access to inputs, particularly in the underserved schools, performance can be expected to go up considerably.

The fact that inefficiency is a less important factor explaining differences in performance should not be taken to mean that there are no efficiency issues affecting primary schools in Togo. As the SDI survey (discussed in Chapter 4) will demonstrate, teachers only spend around 50% of their time teaching. This is an important inefficiency, which needs to be addressed. What the regression analysis suggests is that these inefficiencies affect all schools more or less equally, but also that they might be picked by our control variables. For instance, and we are speculating here, the reason why the presence of more permanent teachers has a negative impact on performance might be because once made permanent, teachers are less motivated to show up and teach. The latter, how to motive teachers, is something to consider carefully, particularly if the Government of Togo is considering the possibility to hire additional permanent teachers.

The results also suggest the importance of paying more attention to the learning environment. The effects can be subtle and are, at times, surprising. Combining the first two classes of primary school has been found to have a positive relation with performance, but combining the last two classes not. Improving teacher quality may also have an important impact on performance, but teacher quality (as expressed through experience or qualifications) is different from hiring permanent teachers. Finally, schools with higher repeating student rates perform worse, and schools that manage to retain more girls perform better.

Appendix

See Table 3.7.

Table 3.7 Summary statistics

Variables	Mean	St. Dev
Number of teachers	5.36	1.86
Teacher students	2.69	1.05
Average qualification teachers*private	0.60	1.07
Private	0.26	0.44
Repeating students rate	0.22	0.12
Ln Average teacher age	3.64	0.13
Female headmaster	0.07	0.26
Female ratio in CM2	0.41	0.15
Average qualification teachers	2.42	0.62
Average student age in CM2	11.91	1.05
Seat every 100 students	82.18	38.65
Desk every 100 students	41.12	19.82
Toilet every 100 students	1.11	1.47
Water	0.35	0.48
Math-book per student	0.34	0.33
Read-book per student	0.49	0.42
CP1-2 taught together	0.22	0.41
CE1-2 taught together	0.35	0.48
CM1-2 taught together	0.45	0.50
Employment rate	70.53	8.72
Employment rate (w/o salary)	87.97	8.75
Dependency ratio	54.53	5.90
Enrollment primary	78.78	7.80
Enrollment secondary	37.04	14.60
Urban	0.26	0.44
Admitted CEPD/Tot students in the school	0.08	0.04
Observations	3957	

References

Aigner, D., C. Lovell, and P. Schmidt. 1977. Formulation and Estimation of Stochastic Frontier Production Function Models. *Journal of Econometrics* 6 (1): 21–37.

Angrist, Joshua D., and Victor Lavy. 1999. Using Maimonides Rule to Estimate the Effect of Class Size on Scholastic Achievement. *Quarterly Journal of Economics* 114 (533): 575.

Banerjee, A., and E. Duflo. 2006. Addressing Absence. *Journal of Economic Perspectives* 20 (1): 117–132.

Case, A., and A. Deaton. 1999. School Inputs and Educational Outcomes in South Africa. *Quarterly Journal of Economics* 114 (3): 1047–1084.

Chaudhury, N., J. Hammer, M. Kremer, K. Muralidharan, and F.H. Rogers. 2006. Missing in Action: Teacher and Health Worker Absence in Developing Countries. *Journal of Economic Perspectives* 20 (1): 91–116.

Duflo, E., R. Hanna, and S.P. Rya. 2012. Incentives Work: Getting Teachers to Come to School. *The American Economic Review* 102 (4): 1241–1278.

Fuchs, T., and L. Woessmann. 2007. What Accounts for International Differences in Student Performance? A Re-examination Using PISA Data. *Empirical Economics* 32 (2–3): 433–464.

Glewwe, P., N. Ilias, and M. Kremer. 2010. Teacher Incentives. *American Economic Journal: Applied Economics* 2 (3): 205–227.

Hanushek, E.A., S. Link, and L. Woessmann. 2013. Does School Autonomy Make Sense Everywhere? Panel Estimates from PISA. *Journal of Development Economics* 104: 212–232.

IMF. 2014. Togo. Poverty Reduction Strategy Paper. IMF Country Report, 14/224.

Kremer, M., N. Chaudhury, F.H. Rogers, K. Muralidharan, and J. Hammer. 2005. Teacher Absence in India: A Snapshot. *Journal of the European Economic Association* 3 (2–3): 658–667.

Krueger, A.B. 1999. Experimental Estimates of Education Production Functions. *Quarterly Journal of Economics* 114 (497): 532.

Madden, G., S. Savage, and S. Kemp. 1997. Measuring Public Sector Efficiency: A Study of Economics Departments at Australian Universities. *Education Economics* 5: 153–168.

Pereira, M.C., and S. Moreira. 2007. A Stochastic Frontier Analysis of Secondary Education Output in Portugal. Working Papers w200706, Banco de Portugal, Economics and Research Department.

Probe Team. 1999. *Public Report on Basic Education in India*. New Delhi: Oxford University Press.

Probe Team. 2011. *Probe Revisited*. New Delhi: Oxford University Press.

Ravallion, M. 2016. *The Economics of Poverty: History, Measurement, and Policy*. New York: Oxford University Press. https://global.oup.com/academic/product/the-economics-of-poverty-9780190212766?cc=us&lang=en&#

Sinuany-Stern, Z., A. Mehrez, and A. Barboy. 1994. Academic Departments Efficiency Via DEA. *Computers & Operations Research* 21: 543–556.

Woessmann, L. 2003. Schooling Resources, Educational Institutions and Student Performance: The International Evidence. *Oxford Bulletin of Economics and Statistics* 65 (2): 117–170.

World Bank. 2004. *World Development Report: Making Services Work for the Poor.* New York: Oxford University Press.

Worthington, A. 2001. An Empirical Survey of Frontier Efficiency Measurement Techniques in Education. *Education Economics* 9 (3): 245–268.

The opinions expressed in this chapter are those of the author(s) and do not necessarily reflect the views of the International Bank for Reconstruction and Development/The World Bank, its Board of Directors, or the countries they represent.

Open Access This chapter is licensed under the terms of the Creative Commons Attribution 3.0 IGO License (https://creativecommons.org/licenses/by/3.0/igo/), which permits use, sharing, adaptation, distribution and reproduction in any medium or format, as long as you give appropriate credit to the International Bank for Reconstruction and Development/The World Bank, provide a link to the Creative Commons license and indicate if changes were made.

The use of the International Bank for Reconstruction and Development/The World Bank's name, and the use of the International Bank for Reconstruction and Development/The World Bank's logo, shall be subject to a separate written license agreement between the International Bank for Reconstruction and Development/The World Bank and the user and is not authorized as part of this CC-IGO license. Note that the link provided above includes additional terms and conditions of the license.

The images or other third party material in this chapter are included in the chapter's Creative Commons license, unless indicated otherwise in a credit line to the material. If material is not included in the chapter's Creative Commons license and your intended use is not permitted by statutory regulation or exceeds the permitted use, you will need to obtain permission directly from the copyright holder.

CHAPTER 4

Student Learning and Teacher Competence

Johannes Hoogeveen, Marcello Matranga
and Mariacristina Rossi

Abstract In this chapter, we analyze individual primary school children learning outcomes, using a unique dataset, the SDI dataset that comprises information about learning achievement for students, schools, and teachers. The novelty of the dataset is the collection of information from teachers, testing their knowledge in math, French, and non-verbal reasoning. Our results show that enrolling in a private school and living in an urban area are associated with better learning outcomes, even when the characteristics of the schools and teachers are controlled for. The results also show a worryingly low level of competency for teachers. Overall, the results point to a deep learning crisis, so deep that serious public action is needed to address it: changes at the margin are unlikely to suffice.

J. Hoogeveen
World Bank, Washington, DC, USA
e-mail: jhoogeveen@worldbank.org

M. Matranga · M. Rossi (✉)
School of Management and Economics, Università di Torino, Turin, Italy
e-mail: marcello.matranga@unito.it

M. Rossi
e-mail: mariacristina.rossi@unito.it

Keywords SDI dataset · Math · French · Non-verbal reasoning · Learning outcomes · Teacher competence

4.1 Introduction to the Chapter

Our goal is to investigate individual learning outcome drivers. This is carried out by using pupils' test scores obtained from an independent learning assessment survey: the Survey and Delivery Indicators (SDI) survey. This is opposed to the way student performance was measured in the previous chapter, where we relied on the results of the end-of-school exam. The SDI dataset captures students and teachers' knowledge data for students in grade four. The data suggests that while enrollment rates have reached unprecedented levels, suggesting enormous progress in human capital accumulation, the picture is less rosy than it may seem at first sight. Many students, it turns out, fail to acquire basic skills, despite attending school. Moreover, many teachers show skill deficiencies.

Key results are illustrated in Table 4.1, which presents summary statistics for public and private schools, with an additional breakdown between urban and rural public schools. Out of a maximum score of 100, students score on average 45.1. Since the SDI test is a grade specific test, one would expect the vast majority of students to score highly, 70–80% or higher—on average! So, these results point toward insufficient learning by pupils who attend primary school. The results hold for both French and mathematics and hold for both private and public institutions, with private schools doing better and rural public schools doing worse.

One of the unique features of the SDI approach is that teacher qualifications are also tested. Since pupils cannot learn more from their teachers than what the teachers know, assessing teacher knowledge is evidently important. Worryingly the average score of teachers was not different than that from their students: 43.0. Among the teachers, only 2.7% scored 80% or higher. In rural public schools, even less than 1% managed to get a score of 80%. Evidently, teacher qualifications are an issue.

Other aspects of the learning environment are not encouraging either. Overall, 21.6% of teachers were not in school during an unannounced visit (a further 15% were at school, but not in the classroom). When in the classroom, teachers taught 79.2% of the time, meaning that nearly

Table 4.1 SDI key results

	Togo	Public	Private	Urban public	Rural public
	2013	2012	2014	2013	2014
Student learning outcomes					
Combined math/language score	45.1	38.4	63.8	46.9	36.0
French score (%)	44.9	37.6	66.3	47.2	34.5
Math score (%)	43.9	41.0	52.1	43.1	40.4
Teacher knowledge					
Minimum knowledge	2.7	1.4	4.8	4.5	0.8
Test score (out of 100)	43.0	40.6	48.6	46.5	39.4
Teacher effort					
School absence rate (% teachers)	21.6	23.0	18.5	14.0	24.3
Classroom absence rate (% teachers)	37.2	38.9	33.3	25.3	41.5
Time spent teaching per day	2 h 40 m	2 h 38 m	2 h 44 m	3 h 13 m	2 h 33 m
Scheduled teaching time per day	5 h 29 m	5 h 28 m	5 h 33 m	5 h 28 m	5 h 28 m
Resource availability					
Student–teacher ratio (observed)	29.1	31.0	24.8	33.5	27.5
Textbook availability (percent of students)	68.5	76.0	52.6	73.3	66.6
Teaching equipment availability (% classrooms)	26.4	24.3	30.8	9.4	27.5
Infrastructure availability (% of schools)	22.3	14.4	39.2	18.6	13.6

Source Adapted from Rockmore (2016). Togo Service Delivery Indicators: Education 2013

one-fifth of the time was devoted to other activities. Cumulating the sources of lost teaching time, pupils have roughly 48.9% of the scheduled teaching time.

In Chapter 2 it was noted how the average student teacher ratio has remained constant at 42–1 since the introduction of free primary education, suggesting that number of teachers increased to accommodate the massive entrance of new pupils since school fees were abolished.

It is not only teachers who are missing from school, so are students. Though the official student teacher ratio is 42–1, the student teacher ratio that was observed was much lower: 29–1. With that, the number of teachers to students actually exceeds the norm of 40–1.

Scholastic inputs are also lacking. This was already pointed out in the previous chapter. There are important input deficiencies that make teaching more difficult. Roughly one-quarter (22.3%) of schools had the minimum infrastructure, primarily because only one school in four has functional, private, and accessible latrines. 14.6% of public schools have the minimum teaching equipment, and textbooks are only available half the time.

Togo's outcomes are not unlike those of other African countries (see Table 4.10) which also show inadequate learning outcomes by pupils, a high fraction of unqualified teachers, a lack of teacher motivation as evidenced by frequent absenteeism and inadequate scholastic and infrastructural inputs. In the remainder of this chapter we use the SDI data to unpack which of the various factors, teacher presence, scholastic materials or teacher knowledge is the key driver of student learning outcomes. The literature suggests a somewhat weak relationship between resources and student performance, which, in turn, has been associated with deficiencies in the incentive structure of school and education systems. Indeed, in Togo incentives for teaching staff are not great, as evidenced by the reliance on temporary staff and teaching assistants/volunteers and the frequent strikes that marred the SDI data collection (http://datatopics.worldbank.org/sdi/). Therefore, scholastic materials alone may have a limited impact on the quality of education, yet it is possible that inputs are complementary to staff motivation, so coupling improvements in both may have significant impacts (see Hanushek 2006). As noted by Duflo et al. (2011), the fact that budgets have not kept pace with enrollment, leading to large pupil–teacher ratios, overstretched physical infrastructure, and insufficient number of textbooks, etc., is problematic. For Togo this is not entirely the case as budgets did keep pace with increases in enrollment. Yet while student teacher ratios did not increase, infrastructure deficits remain huge. However, simply increasing the level of resources might not address the quality deficit in education without also taking teachers' incentives and qualifications into account. In fact, we find that if only one thing can be addressed through public policy making, teacher knowledge should be given the priority. Before turning to the analysis, however, we first present the SDI data.

4.2 SDI Data

To date, there is no standardized set of indicators, at least not for Africa, to measure the quality of education. The SDI surveys attempt to fill this gap by providing a homogenous set of indicators for several countries, on learning outcomes as well as facilities and teachers characteristics. The datasets are collected over time, enabling governments and service provider to track progress within and across countries over time.[1]

The SDI data for Togo were collected in 2013 from a representative sample of 200 primary schools, 1141 teachers, and 1938 grade four pupils. To get a reliable measure of teacher presence, schools were visited twice, each time unannounced. During the period of data collection, there were a number of strikes, both by civil servants and employees of faith-based schools that were felt differently in rural and urban areas and the SDI results reflect these realities. First visits were reprogrammed to the extent possible so that teams conducted the first visits on days when there were no strikes. However, second visits were allowed to fall on strike days to reflect the reality faced by pupils (Rockmore 2016).

The results provide a representative snapshot of the quality of service delivery and the physical environment within which services are delivered in public primary schools. In addition to information about student knowledge, the SDI provides information on three levels of service delivery: measures of (i) teacher effort; (ii) teacher knowledge and ability; and (iii) the availability of key inputs, such as textbooks, basic teaching equipment, and infrastructure (such as sanitation, quality of lighting etc.). The test used to assess the pupils' level of knowledge is a standard, grade specific test. The SDI survey instrument was adapted to the Togolese context through a participatory process involving technical discussions, training, and piloting with the Ministry of Education's National (Education) Evaluation Commission (*Commission nationale d'évaluation*; CNE). The tests assess the ability to do basic reading and arithmetic through a test articulated in three main sections: French, mathematics, and non-verbal reasoning. In the French vocabulary task, for instance, the pupils have to know the correct French words for four subjects drawn as pictures (a tree, an elephant, a pair of shoes, a t-shirt); in the ordering number task pupils should rank in ascending order a series of six number below 1000;

---

[1] See also http://siteresources.worldbank.org/AFRICAEXT/Resources/What_is_SDI.pdf.

finally, the non-verbal reasoning section is composed by four simple exercises where the pupils are asked to choose among a series of geometrical figures or patterns having different shape, color, and texture which one among the six options available would fit with those stated as in the questions. More detail about the SDI test can be found in Box 4.1.

Box 4.1 SDI test

Pupils tests

French

Reading–decoding exercises:
Pupils' reading and decoding skills, as well as the knowledge of French vocabulary, are tested through exercises based on graphological and iconographical identification:
- Letter recognition: pupils are asked to be able to identify a specific letter among a set of nine (the exercise is repeated three times)
- Word recognition: pupils are asked to be able to identify a specific French word among a set of nine (the exercise is repeated three times)
- Vocabulary: pupils are asked to be able to state the correct French words for four subjects drawn as pictures (a tree, an elephant, a pair of shoes, a t-shirt)

Reading comprehension exercises:
- Reading Short Sentence: pupils are asked to be able to correctly read aloud a short sentence eight words long
- Reading Long Sentence: pupils are asked to be able to correctly read aloud a long sentence seventy words long
- Reading Comprehension: pupils are asked to answer to three simple questions about the long sentence previously read

Mathematics

Numbers:
Pupils' basic arithmetic skills are tested through exercises based on counting, numbers recognition, and ranking:
- Number Recognition: pupils are asked to be able to identify a specific number among a set of nine (the exercise is repeated three times)
- Ordering Numbers: pupils are asked to be able to rank in ascending order a series of six number below 1000

Pupils tests

Four basic operations:
Pupils' basic arithmetic skills are tested through exercises based on the four basic operations (addition, subtraction, multiplication, division)
- Single-digit Addition
- Double-digit Addition
- Triple-digit Addition
- Single-digit Subtraction
- Double-digit Subtraction
- Single-digit Multiplication
- Double-digit Multiplication
- Triple-digit Multiplication
- Single-digit Division A
- Single-digit Division B

Analytical skills:
Pupils' analytical skills are tested through exercises which require a combination of critical thinking and basic arithmetic skills
- Comparing Ratios: pupils are asked to be able to compare the results of three ratios
- Problem Solving A: pupils are asked to be able to solve a problem which requires the use of multiplication
- Problem Solving B: pupils are asked to be able to identify the number that will follow in a sequence of four numbers

Non-verbal reasoning

Logic:
Pupils' reasoning abilities are tested through a series of four puzzles
- Shape Recognition A: pupils are asked to be able to choose among six geometrical figures or signs having different shape, color, and texture which figure or sign would be fit to complete the sequence of four
- Shape Recognition B: pupils are asked to be able to choose among six geometrical figures or signs having different shape, color, and texture which figure or sign would be fit to complete the sequence of four
- Pattern Recognition A: pupils are asked to be able to choose among six geometrical figures or signs having different shape, color, and texture which figure or sign would be fit to complete the sequence of four
- Pattern Recognition B: pupils are asked to be able to choose among six geometrical figures or signs having different shape, color, and texture which figure or sign would be fit to complete the sequence of four

4.3 Descriptive Evidence

4.3.1 Pupils' Knowledge

To provide a meaningful but compact snapshot of the pupils' general knowledge, we decided to select, as four key indicators, the average score to the vocabulary question, the joint non-verbal reasoning exercises, the single-digit multiplication, and the double-digit multiplication questions. Table 4.2 summarizes the average score in percentage points for the specific questions asked in each section. Table 4.4 illustrates the ratio of pupils with correct answers by region and rural areas.

Looking at the mathematical skills (Table 4.2) the poor performance by pupils is striking. Ordering number is known by only half the students. Results are (somewhat surprising) better for the percentage of pupils able to do single-digit addition. The lowest and dramatic score is on double-digit multiplication, which shows that pupils do not know the method to solve the operation, when the operation cannot be solved using one's own fingers.

Pupils' average test score in non-verbal reasoning is particularly homogeneous both across regions and area if compared to the other key indicators. Table 4.4 shows that there is no relevant difference in average score computed in specific regions or area with the only exceptions of Savanes, Kara and Plateaux where, on average, children perform slightly worse than their peers who live in other regions.

A look at the distribution (Fig. 4.1) of the pupils' score reveals a distribution across private schools mirroring that in public schools, with private schools showing a much higher ratio of pupils with higher scores. The differences in pupils' test score between public and private schools are largely driven by the results of the French test: a possible explanation could be the fact that children going to private school are more likely to speak (or be exposed to) French at home given that may come from wealthier and more educated family backgrounds (Figs. 4.2, 4.3 and 5.2) and most likely they live in Lomé. This explanation is reinforced by the finding that teachers in public and private schools do about equally well on the French test (Table 4.5).

The distribution of math scores (Fig. 4.3) is less skewed than the total one, showing a bigger mass at central values, with a vast majority whose

Table 4.2 Descriptive SDI test results

Mathematics		Non-verbal reasoning	
Variable	Mean	Variable	Mean
Number Recognition	98.45	Shape Recognition A[2]	88.22
Ordering Numbers	52.60	Shape Recognition B	77.76
Single-digit Addition	76.47	Pattern Recognition A[3]	38.79
Double-digit Addition	64.63	Pattern Recognition B	7.98
Triple-digit Addition	64.57	Total non-verbal Reasoning	53.18
Single-digit Subtraction	64.47		
Double-digit Subtraction	20.77	*French*	
Single-digit Multiplication	10.53	Variable	Mean
Double-digit Multiplication	5.31	Letter Recognition	89.35
Triple-digit Multiplication	4.31	Word Recognition	77.17
Single-digit Division A[1]	35.05	Vocabulary	65.15
Single-digit Division B	11.11	Reading Short Sentence	42.38
Comparing Ratios	19.32	Reading Long Sentence	41.98
Problem Solving A	9.12	Reading Comprehension	16.89
Problem Solving B	13.18		

Weighted Average Score in percentage points. Division in ([1]) A: one-digit number divided and one-digit number divisor B: two-digit number dividend and one-digit number divisor
Source Our elaborations on SDI data

math score is below 50% in public schools, the picture is again mirrored in private schools, albeit more centered toward the middle of the distribution. The average score distribution shows a marked difference in the distribution, as well as in the average values as previously shown. Public schools show an alarmingly large number of pupils with around zero scores while this evidence is not present at this extent in the private schools. This evidence shows that there is a significant group of pupils who are not learning at all.

Finally, Table 4.3 provides a snapshot of the correlation existing among the scores achieved by pupils in the three subjects. Although statistically significant different from zero the correlations among test scores widely differ across areas, showing the highest correlation between French and math (around 60%), while the correlation is lower between non-verbal reasoning and math (and French too), not reaching 20%. It suggests that non-verbal reasoning measures something that is very different from math and French.

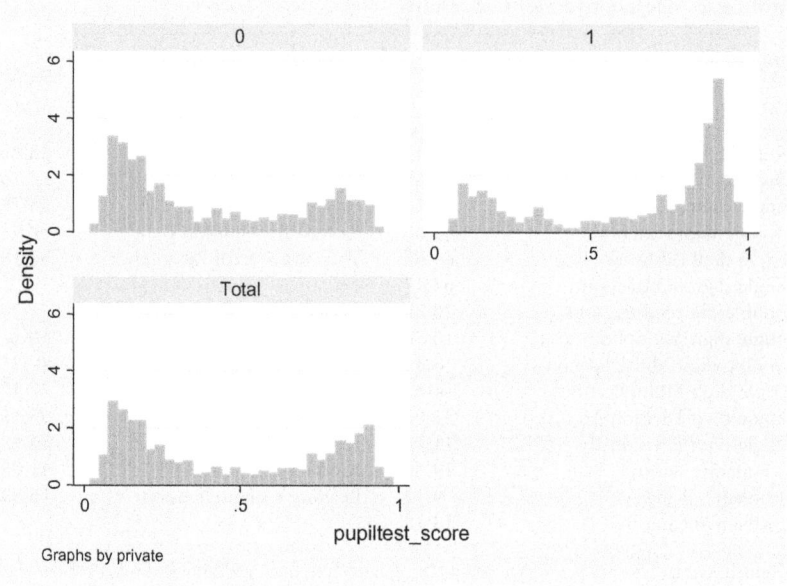

Fig. 4.1 Distribution of pupils' average scores across public (0) and private (1) (*Source* Authors' calculations using SDI data)

4.3.2 Regional Differences

Irrespective of test score, urban areas always do better than rural areas and pupils in the Golfe-Lomé region always outperform those in other regions (note however, that this region is also almost entirely urban and with a high prevalence of private schools). With regard to the French vocabulary question (Table 4.4), which tested the ability of pupils to write the French word for four different pictures, pupils attending a school located in an urban area perform better than the other ones. In terms of regions, on average, children located in the mostly urban Golfe Lomé outperform the national average (88.2 percentage points against 65.2 percentage points). With respect to math (single or double-digit multiplication) pupils in Golfe-Lomé score higher (16.4% for single-digit multiplication; 15.6% of double-digit multiplication) than those in any other region. Particularly for double-digit multiplication the difference is stark as there is no region where more than 5% manage to successfully

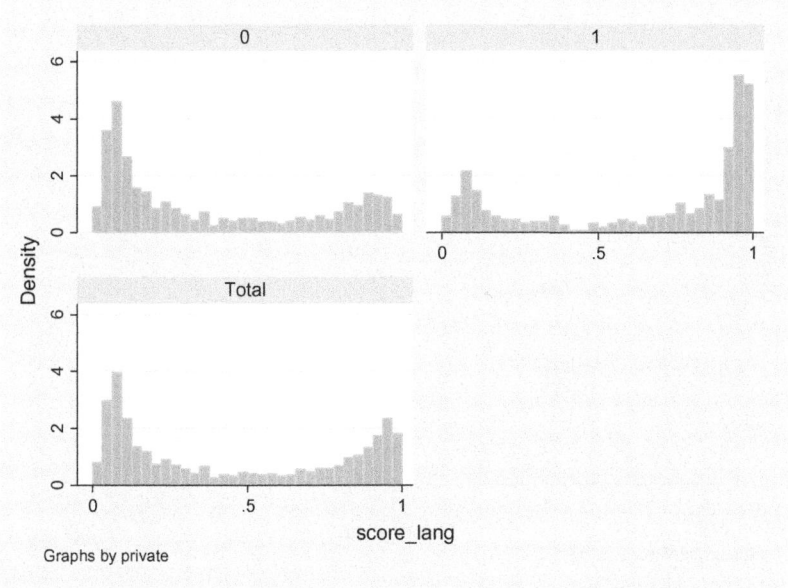

Fig. 4.2 Distribution of pupils' French test scores (*Source* Authors' calculations using SDI data)

complete double-digit multiplication. That said, even the score for Lomé is dismal. The difference in score for non-verbal reasoning is relatively small, with all regions scoring between 47 and 57 percentage points. The superior performance of Golfe-Lomé is much stronger for vocabulary than for maths, and least for non-verbal reasoning, suggesting that the main difference with other regions (and between urban and rural areas) is language related rather than differences in analytic skills or reasoning.

4.3.3 Teachers Knowledge

The unique feature of this dataset allows researchers to know the scores for teachers as well as for students. Teachers were tested with similar questions administered to students, at a slightly higher level of difficulty. The average scores show an impressively low level, with mathematical knowledge standing slightly below of 35% of correct responses. Expecting that a teacher should master the taught subject, an average

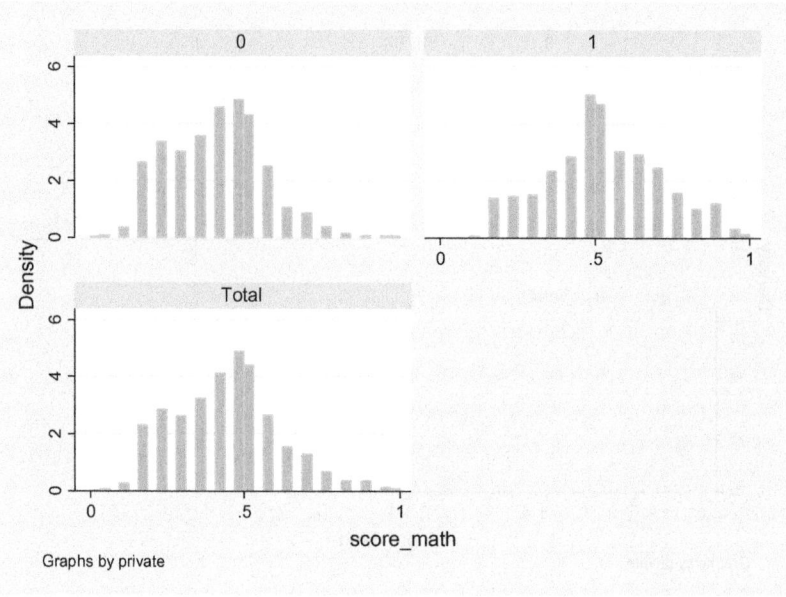

Fig. 4.3 Distribution of pupils' math test scores (*Source* Authors' calculations using SDI data)

Table 4.3 Test score correlations

	Score French test	Score math test
Score math test	0.5837*	
	0.0000	
Non-verbal reasoning test	0.1786*	0.1989*
	0.0000	0.0000

Source Authors' calculations using SDI data
*$p<0.1$, **$p<0.05$, ***$p<0.01$

level of 80% (70% if you would like to be less ambitious) could safely be considered a lower threshold. The level of teachers' knowledge is general poor showing particularly low level in mathematical and pedagogical skills (see Filmer, Molina, et al. 2017). In Table 4.5 we show the average values by urban/rural and private/public schools. Difference in knowledge of French does not show up overall, suggesting that the level of

Table 4.4 SDI test scores of pupils by region and rural and urban areas

	Vocabulary	Non-verbal reasoning	Single-digit multiplication	Double-digit multiplication
Golfe-Lomé	88.18	57.84	16.35	15.57
	(0.19)	(17.61)	(37.02)	(36.29)
Maritime	56.50	55.13	8.25	5.41
	(30.09)	(19.01)	(27.55)	(22.64)
Plateaux	61.28	47.11	12.78	2.16
	(28.96)	(23.02)	(33.43)	(14.54)
Centrale	63.30	56.84	9.43	2.49
	(28.71)	(22.55)	(29.30)	(15.62)
Kara	57.38	53.19	7.64	2.76
	(31.32)	(19.26)	(26.63)	(16.42)
Savanes	62.92	49.14	6.99	0.81
	(28.03)	(23.60)	(25.55)	(8.97)
Togo	65.15	53.18	10.53	5.31
	(30.13)	(21.11)	(30.70)	(22.43)
Rural	58.28	51.85	9.30	3.37
	(29.43)	(21.90)	(29.05)	(18.06)
Urban	80.71	56.22	13.32	9.71
	(25.58)	(18.89)	(34.01)	(29.63)

Variable which takes value between 0 and 1 according the fraction of correct answers to the vocabulary exercises. Percentage points, weighted results
Source Authors' calculations using SDI data

knowledge of teachers does not differ widely. A remarkably low ratio of teachers has more than 70% of answers correct, a percentage of 13% in French and 15% in math. These numbers vary across schools, ranging from 17% in French in urban schools to 11% in rural schools.

The SDI dataset allows to further break down the urban/rural dimension across different regions (Table 4.6). As was the case for pupil test scores, teachers in Golfe-Lomé and teachers in urban areas score better than teachers in all other regions or those in rural areas. However, unlike the pupil test score, the French knowledge of teachers is substantially uniform (around 50 percentage points) across regions, and only slightly better in urban areas than in rural areas.

As previously demonstrated, teachers' mathematical skills are quite poor. By looking at regional differences it can be seen how teachers located in the Golfe-Lomé region outperform their colleagues living in other regions of the country (43.1 percentage points against a national

Table 4.5 Distribution of teachers' test scores

	Total	Public	Private	% Diff. (public–private)	Urban	Rural	% Diff. (urban–rural)
Math	33.4	31.1	38.1	−22.5***	41.2	29.9	27.5***
French	50.9	49.6	53.7	−8.2**	53.5	49.7	7.1**
Math >70%	15.3	13.1	19.7	−50.2**	24.5	11.0	54.8***
French >70%	13.5	12.2	16.1	−32.1	17.2	11.8	31.5**

Source Authors' calculations using SDI data
$*p<0.1, **p<0.05, ***p<0.01$

average of 33.4 percentage points). Also, in this case, almost all urban areas perform better than the rural ones.

The teachers' questionnaire contains a section dedicated to investigate their pedagogical skills; the range of exercises and questions asked help providing a snapshot of teachers' ability to prepare and organize lessons, assess children's ability, and evaluate students' progress. Results from these questions are not encouraging. Teachers' pedagogical knowledge is disturbingly low: the average ratio of correct answers (expressed in percentage points) varies from 15.8 of Plateaux region to 22.1 of Savanes with the national average reaching only 19.6 (Table 4.6).

4.4 Analysis of Variance

It might be interesting to investigate to which degree the variation in pupils' test scores is driven by school level (including teacher qualification) and individual level-characteristics. To explore this, we use a standard Analysis of Variance (ANOVA) model. The ANOVA model let us understand whether it is possible to claim that there is no significant difference in the means of pupils' test score at school level, which makes the use of multivariate analysis important to detect the relevance of different drivers. It must be noticed that, since to the SDI dataset is based on information collected from 1938 grade four pupils randomly selected among 200 randomly selected school in Togo, the model takes form of One-way random effects ANOVA and then the results can be generalized back to the entire population (Table 4.7).

For each of the three tests the "Between Groups" line refers to the variation of the school mean around the population mean, the "Within Groups" line refers to the variation of the pupils' scores around their

Table 4.6 SDI test scores for teachers by region and rural and urban areas

	French	Math	Double-digit multiplication	Pedagogical
Golfe-Lomé	52.38	43.14	59.00	20.38
	(15.01)	(26.20)	(49.30)	(13.48)
Maritime	51.65	35.17	52.65	22.10
	(15.86)	(25.39)	(50.09)	(16.94)
Plateaux	51.27	33.20	56.14	15.75
	(17.18)	(21.79)	(49.77)	(13.06)
Centrale	50.41	18.49	33.81	16.45
	(19.35)	(18.78)	(47.55)	(11.72)
Kara	47.72	21.73	37.45	21.07
	(16.21)	(22.71)	(48.70)	(14.50)
Savanes	49.59	37.57	52.66	22.08
	(17.14)	(28.71)	(50.16)	(18.01)
Total	50.90	33.36	50.90	19.61
	(16.61)	(25.55)	(50.02)	(14.95)
Rural	49.72	29.71	46.91	19.03
	(16.85)	(24.44)	(49.95)	(14.98)
Urban	53.48	41.36	59.65	20.89
	(15.79)	(26.14)	(49.15)	(14.85)

Source Authors' calculations using SDI data

Table 4.7 Analysis of variance of SDI test scores

Analysis of variance—ANOVA

	Source	Sum of squares (SS)	Df	Mean square (MS)	F	Prob > F
ANOVA French test score	Between groups	121.5492	194	0.6265	8.30	0.0000
	Within groups	131.5854	1743	0.0755		
	Total	253.1346	1937	0.1307		
ANOVA Math test score	Between groups	24.1346	194	0.1244	6.83	0.0000
	Within groups	31.7302	1743	0.0182		
	Total	55.8649	1937	0.0288		
ANOVA Non-verbal reasoning test score	Between groups	17.9613	194	0.0926	2.31	0.0000
	Within groups	69.7676	1743	0.0400		
	Total	87.7289	1937	0.0453		

Source Authors' calculations using SDI data

school mean, and the "Total" line refers to the variation of the pupils' scores around the population mean. The F-statistics are given by the ratio between the groups Mean Square (MS) and within groups MS. In all the three case the null hypothesis that the average value of the dependent variable is the same for all groups is rejected; the within group MS is definitively smaller than the between group MS. This suggests that the differences between test scores are not solely explained by differences between students and confirms the relevance of school levels characteristics (including teacher qualifications) in explaining pupils' test scores.

4.5 Regression Analysis

In this section we present the results of our regression analysis where we investigate how each factor affects pupil scores in math, French, and Non-Verbal Reasoning. We consider as dependent variable the scores in these topics (100% is the maximum score with all correct answers).

Multivariate analysis allows us to control for each factor, keeping other determinants constant, which allows us to purge our results by possible contamination with other inter-related factors.

Results are presented in Table 4.9.

Starting with the gender of the student, results show that scores are lower for girls, despite being significant in mathematics only. Pupil teacher ratios do not have the same impact on the three subjects. Larger classes have a negative effect on performance in French while it has a small and positive effect on non-verbal reasoning. Class size is not significant in mathematics. Remarkably, absenteeism of teachers does not affect the final score results nor does teacher experience; having an assistant/volunteer teacher, on the other hand, is a critical driver, particularly in French. The presence of assistant teachers shows the highest (negative) impact, by decreasing French marks by 60 percentage points versus five in mathematics. The availability of books does matter with the exception of non-verbal reasoning where it is not significant. Interestingly, book availability has a higher impact for French than for math, suggesting that improving performance by simple providing additional text books is more difficult in conceptual topics like mathematics. In fact, the results suggest that the way to address improvements in test scores may vary by subject. For a subject like math, having a text book is as important as having a qualified teacher. For French, having a qualified teacher is much more critical than the availability of textbooks.

Table 4.8 Summary of variables used in the regression analysis

Variable	Mean	Std. Dev.
Dependent variables		
Pupils' mathematics score	44.48	16.98
Pupils' French score	45.38	36.15
Pupils' non-verbal reasoning score	53.47	21.28
Independent variables		
Female	0.51	0.50
Urban	0.31	0.46
Private	0.26	0.44
Pupil–teacher ratio	48.09	16.17
Toilets	0.57	0.49
Presence at school (rate) of non-assistant teachers	0.22	0.28
Multi-grade classes	0.39	0.49
Pupil had breakfast	0.73	0.44
Number of classrooms	6.38	2.58
Share of pupils with pencils	0.88	0.17
Share of female teachers	0.18	0.20
Share of assistant/volunteer teachers	0.32	0.26
Average years of education of teachers	6.86	0.87
Average years of teaching	12.02	4.30
Parents' association	1.07	0.26
Number of meetings	1.23	0.63
Share of pupils with mathematics textbook	0.66	0.34
Share of pupils with French textbook	0.73	0.32
Share of pupils with textbook	0.69	0.34

Source Authors' calculations using SDI data

Multivariate analysis confirms what was reported earlier that better learning outcomes are found in private schools, with private schools exhibiting the highest coefficients: students at private schools score 9 percentage points more in their math test than their public-school peers; in French the gap is the highest with 20 percentage points of difference. Let us remind the reader that our dataset does not collect information on parental background, including wealth. Attending a private school versus a public one could be endogenously driven by the wealth of the family. Given these features of the data, the private school effect is likely to be driven by a wealth effect, rather than a school effect. Students coming from richer families are more likely to go to private schools (Fig. 5.2). Controlling for the quality of teachers, private schools perform better, which can be easily explained by the demand side rather than by the quality of supply (which is controlled for). The gap is larger in French, which is also a better proxy for belonging to richer families, more exposed to French language.

It is worth remarking that the ratio of female teachers positively affects the performance, with the exception of math, this probably suggesting additional effort, which cannot be controlled by regression analysis being unobserved. Since the ratio of female staff in public schools is only 14%, this is another area for attention.

Some of the school inputs that traditionally get quite some attention from donors, such as toilets or whether a child had breakfast (school feeding) do not seem to affect test scores. Surprisingly, parental associations matter in a negative way, even after controlling for the frequency of the meetings. This could be explained by the endogeneity of the variable. Parental associations are a choice variable, and they could be more likely to occur when student results are poor, or in isolated (rural) areas where the only schools available are (former) local initiative schools (EDIL) which were started and run by parents (Table 4.9).

4.6 Concluding Remarks

The SDI results for Togo are not out of line of those for other countries in the region. These countries too, face inadequate student learning, unqualified teachers, low teacher motivation, and insufficient scholastic and infrastructural resources. Clearly there are differences attributable to country specificities though. Learning outcomes are better in Kenya, for instance, even though the average time spent by teachers in Kenya is comparable to that in other countries (see Table 4.10).

One of the consequences of the free education program in Togo seems to have been that many ill-qualified assistant teachers entered the school system. And as Table 2.2 demonstrates, the hiring of temporary staff and teaching assistants has continued since. After all, within the public school system there is a strong reliance on teaching assistants and temporary staff, staff getting paid half, or less than half, compared to what their civil servant colleagues make and who make up 60% of the staff complement. Yet this is not the entire story. When only 2.7% of teachers can satisfactorily complete their test, the 40% of teachers who are civil servants and who presumable completed their training at teacher colleges are deficient in their knowledge too!

Table 4.9 Regression analysis on pupils' scores

	(1) Math b/se	(2) French b/se	(3) NVR b/se
Female pupil	−4.546*** (0.848)	−3.689 (2.502)	−0.922 (0.991)
Urban-school	0.687 (1.227)	−8.381** (3.906)	1.392 (1.383)
Private-school	8.515*** (1.332)	20.018*** (4.196)	0.797 (1.504)
Pupil teacher ratio	−0.021 (0.029)	−0.205** (0.097)	0.055* (0.034)
Toilet	−1.749 (1.069)	−1.504 (3.595)	−2.274* (1.224)
Presence at school of non-assistant teachers	3.246** (1.632)	−8.172 (5.449)	0.010 (1.868)
Multi-grade classes	0.282 (1.034)	−0.886 (4.130)	−3.180** (1.243)
Pupil had breakfast	−0.231 (0.993)	2.935 (2.813)	0.090 (1.139)
Number of classrooms	0.859*** (0.192)	−0.907 (0.756)	0.143 (0.226)
Share of students with pencil	3.108 (3.032)	1.861 (8.080)	−1.846 (3.299)
Share of female teacher	−1.742 (2.629)	15.236** (7.422)	6.659** (2.926)
Share of assistant/volunteer teachers	−5.053** (2.368)	−59.139*** (8.411)	−2.874 (2.814)
Average years of education teacher	1.995*** (0.609)	2.425 (2.083)	0.922 (0.732)
Average years of teaching	0.211* (0.112)	−0.405 (0.406)	−0.149 (0.135)
Parent association	−3.917* (2.291)	−5.270 (4.690)	−3.786* (2.184)
Number of meetings	0.036 (0.821)	−1.934 (2.476)	−0.345 (0.945)
Share of pupils with math textbook	7.449*** (1.510)		
Share of pupils with French textbook		12.247*** (4.394)	
Share of pupils with textbook			0.662 (1.715)
N	1233.000	605.000	1838.000

Source Authors' calculations using SDI data
Marginal effects reported, change in dependent variable is reported when the regressor is a dummy
*$p<0.1$, **$p<0.05$, ***$p<0.01$

The evidence shown in this chapter points at a weakness of the system that goes beyond the marginal impact of some factors. Indeed, average values of pupils' learning outcomes shown in this chapter point toward such an insufficiency in the level of learning, such a deep learning crisis, that it needs massive public action to address, and not by changes at the margin. Looking at the most effective forces behind learning outcomes, two factors stand out as pivotal: private school attendance and the low presence of teaching assistants or volunteers. Whereas the former can plausibly be attributed to demand forces i.e. family background, the latter relates to supply dynamics. Teachers qualifications mirror, indeed, school public investment into human capital. Private school attendance, conversely, reveals a parental choice, which hides the family welfare, better off households more likely to send their kids to private schools. This is particularly consistent across all outcomes, while other factors, when relevant, are often limited to having an impact on outcome. Private school attendance can offset the negative factors such as higher presence of voluntary teachers, by suggesting that wealth effect of the parent can neutralize the negative supply side effect.

Appendix

Regression Variables Description

Dependent Variables

Pupils' mathematics score (total_math_score): variable which defines the pupils' total score in the math section, it is expressed in percentage points

Pupils' French score (total_lang_score): variable which defines the pupils' total score in the French section, it is expressed in percentage points

Pupils' non-verbal reasoning (total_nvr_score): variable which defines the pupils' total score in the non-verbal reasoning section, it is expressed in percentage points.

Independent Variables

Female (female): dummy variable which takes value 1 if the pupil is girl and 0 otherwise

Urban (urban): dummy variable which takes value 1 if the school is located in an urban area and 0 otherwise

Private (private): dummy variable which takes value 1 if the school is private and 0 otherwise

Pupil–Teacher Ratio (pupil teacher ratio): variable which defines the number of students per teacher (values from 0 to 113)

Toilets (toilet): dummy variable which takes value 1 if the school has toilets and 0 otherwise

Presence rate non-assistant teachers: variable which defines the percentage of the non-assistant teacher is present at school, values from 0 to 1

Multi-grade classes: dummy variable taking value 1 if in the school there are multi-grade classes (our elaboration)

Student had Breakfast: dummy variable taking value 1 if the child had breakfast and 0 otherwise (our elaboration)

Number of classroom: number of classrooms in the school has (values from 0 to 20)

Share of pupils with pencils: variable which defines the percentage of pupils having a pencil in a given school, values from 0 to 1

Share of female teachers: variable which defines the percentage of female teachers within each school, values from 0 to 1 (our elaboration)

Share of teachers: variable which defines the percentage of volunteer teachers within each school, values from 0 to 1 (our elaboration)

Average years of education of teachers: variable which defines how many years of education have on average the teachers in a given school, values from 4.33 to 9 (our elaboration)

Average years of teaching: variable which defines by how many years on average the teachers teach in a given school, values from 2.25 to 25.375 (our elaboration)

Parents' association: dummy variable which takes value 1 if in the school is active a parents' association and 0 otherwise

Number of meetings: variable (in logarithm) which describes the number of meetings held by parents' association during the year

Share of pupils with mathematics textbook: variable which defines the percentage of students having a mathematics textbook in a given school, values from 0 to 1

Share of pupils with French textbook: variable defining the percentage of students having a French textbook in a given school, values from 0 to 1

Share of pupils with textbook: variable defining the percentage of students having a textbook in a given school, values from 0 to 1.

Table 4.10 Key SDI results for schools in Togo and selected African countries

	Togo	Kenya	Mozambique	Nigeria	Tanzania	Uganda
	2013	2012	2014	2015	2014	2013
Teacher knowledge (4th grade)						
Minimum knowledge	1.6	40.4	0.3	0.0	21.5	19.5
Test score (out of 100)	35.6	57.1	26.9	33.3	48.3	45.3
Teacher effort						
School absence rate (% teachers)	20.5	14.1	44.8	16.6	14.4	26.0
Classroom absence rate (% teachers)	35.8	42.1	56.2	27.0	46.7	52.8
Time spent teaching per day	3 h 29 m	2 h 49 m	1 h 41 m	4 h 23 m	2 h 46 m	3 h 18 m
Scheduled teaching time per day	5 h 29 m	5 h 37 m	4 h 17 m	5 h 40 m	5 h 54 m	7 h 18 m
Resource availability						
Student–teacher ratio (observed)	29.7	35.2	21.4	38.1	43.5	47.9
Textbook availability (percent of students)	68.5	48.0	68.1	8.7	25.3	5.0
Teaching equipment availability (% classrooms)	26.4	78.8	76.8	23.4	61.4	80.6

(Continued)

Table 4.10 (Continued)

	Togo	Kenya	Mozambique	Nigeria	Tanzania	Uganda
	2013	2012	2014	2015	2014	2013
Infrastructure availability (% of schools)	22.3	59.5	29.1	19.7	40.4	53.7
Student learning outcomes						
Combined math/language score	45.7	72.0	20.8	21.3	40.1+*	48.6
French score (%)	45.5	75.4	18.7	21.7	36.5+*	47.1
Math score (%)	44.6	59.0	25.1	11.5	58.2	43.4

Source Adapted and updated from Rockmore (2016). Togo SDI Report, page i
Note Values for Nigeria are the weighted average of the four states surveyed: Anambra, Bauchi, Ekiti, and Niger. These statistics reflect the updated SDI methodology. Data for Mozambique are for the public sector

REFERENCES

Bold, Tessa, Deon Filmer, Gayle Martin, Ezequiel Molina, Brian Stacy, Christophe Rockmore, Jakob Svensson, and Waly Wane. 2017. Enrollment Without Learning: Teacher Effort, Knowledge, and Skill in Primary Schools in Africa. *Journal of Economic Perspectives* 31 (4): 185–204.

Duflo, E., P. Dupas, and M. Kremer. 2011. Peer Effects, Teacher Incentives, and the Impact of Tracking: Evidence from a Randomized Evaluation in Kenya. *American Economic Review* 101 (5): 1739–1774.

Hanushek, E. 2006. Alternative School Policies and the Benefits of General Cognitive Skills. *Economics of Education Review* 25 (4): 447–462.

Rockmore, Christopher. 2016. Togo Service Delivery Indicators: Education 2013. The World Bank. http://microdata.worldbank.org/index.php/catalog/2753/.

The opinions expressed in this chapter are those of the author(s) and do not necessarily reflect the views of the International Bank for Reconstruction and Development/The World Bank, its Board of Directors, or the countries they represent.

Open Access This chapter is licensed under the terms of the Creative Commons Attribution 3.0 IGO License (https://creativecommons.org/licenses/by/3.0/igo/), which permits use, sharing, adaptation, distribution and reproduction in any medium or format, as long as you give appropriate credit to the International Bank for Reconstruction and Development/The World Bank, provide a link to the Creative Commons license and indicate if changes were made.

The use of the International Bank for Reconstruction and Development/The World Bank's name, and the use of the International Bank for Reconstruction and Development/The World Bank's logo, shall be subject to a separate written license agreement between the International Bank for Reconstruction and Development/The World Bank and the user and is not authorized as part of this CC-IGO license. Note that the link provided above includes additional terms and conditions of the license.

The images or other third party material in this chapter are included in the chapter's Creative Commons license, unless indicated otherwise in a credit line to the material. If material is not included in the chapter's Creative Commons license and your intended use is not permitted by statutory regulation or exceeds the permitted use, you will need to obtain permission directly from the copyright holder.

CHAPTER 5

Policy Suggestions and Concluding Remarks

Johannes Hoogeveen and Mariacristina Rossi

Abstract In this concluding chapter, we summarize the main findings and offer policy suggestions. As the outcome of inadequate learning goes hand in hand with the poor quality of teaching, policy interventions have to embrace programs that radically address the problem. Marginal policies by themselves are unlikely to be sufficient but can be combined with intensive programs aimed at reversing the inadequate learning outcomes. Identifying successful programs is likely to require an involved search process of trying different approaches and scaling up what works best.

Keywords Policy suggestions · Learning outcomes · Teacher competence · Iterative intervention design

J. Hoogeveen (✉)
World Bank, Washington, DC, USA
e-mail: jhoogeveen@worldbank.org

M. Rossi
School of Management and Economics, Università di Torino, Turin, Italy
e-mail: mariacristina.rossi@unito.it

5.1 Summary of Main Findings

In the course of this book, evidence was presented on the state of learning by primary school students in Togo. We made use of several data sets, both administrative and survey microdata. Irrespective of the source used, the available data suggest that the abolishment of school fees improved access considerably, particularly in the first year. In 2008/2009 enrollment in public schools increased by some 30%, an increase that had significant equalizing effects in that many more relatively disadvantaged children, girls, those from poorer households, those living in rural areas, or those living in the far north, ended up going to school.

While the achievements in terms of school access and inequality reduction are noteworthy, learning outcomes are unequivocally poor. The majority of students do not perform adequately when tested on math or French. Just to illustrate how bad the situation is, only 53% of students in grade four know how to order six random numbers under 1000. In the absence of such basic knowledge, it seems plausible that an entire generation of children may grow into adults who participate in the labor market and in civil society, without being equipped with even the most rudimentary academic skills.

Another way to highlight the depth of the learning crisis is by considering performance at the level of schools. We do so in Fig. 5.1, which shows the percent of schools in which at least 70% of answers were given correctly on a grade-specific math test. As the graph shows, most schools have zero students who get 70% correct answers. In only 3% of the schools is more than half of students able to get at least a score of 70%. In other words, almost all schools fail their students entirely.

These results are particularly dramatic considering that spending on education increased significantly. Expressed as fraction of GDP spending on education almost doubled from 1.3% of GDP in 2006 to 2.4% in 2015; expressed on a per-student basis spending went up from FCFA 24,000 in 2006 to FCFA 43,000 in 2015. It suggests that the investments government is making in public education is a poor one, something that many parents seem to have realized. Because, despite public primary education having become free and available for all, the fraction of children opting to go to nonpublic schools has remained unequivocally high: around 30%.

In an effort to explore pathways toward improving learning outcomes, this book explored correlates of learning outcomes. We found that

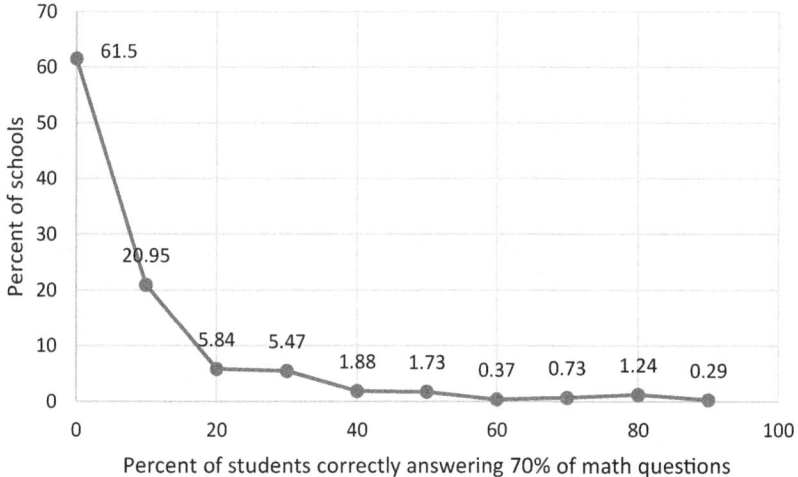

Fig. 5.1 Percent schools by percent of students that answers at least 70% of math questions correctly (*Source* Authors' calculations using SDI data)

certain policies are likely to improve outcomes at the margin: a better balancing of teachers and scholastic inputs across schools would reduce inequalities and improve efficiency and performance; stimulating involvement of parents in the school could enhance the motivation of students and teachers. One noteworthy finding is that private schools perform better than public ones, a performance that helps explain why so many parents opt to send their children to nonpublic (religious or laic) schools. The better performance of private schools remained even after controlling for the (slightly) higher quality of teachers engaged in private schools.[1] In other words, there are other factors, in addition to better-trained teachers, that make students in private schools perform better. We suggest that a combination of selection effects rooted in higher motivation and more capable students are plausible reasons for explaining these results. Parents who pay for a private education of their children are more likely to motivate their children, and their children's teachers, to perform. This effect is corroborated by the fact that the parents

---

[1] Note though that while private schools perform better, their learning outcomes tend to be below the threshold, but only less so than public schools.

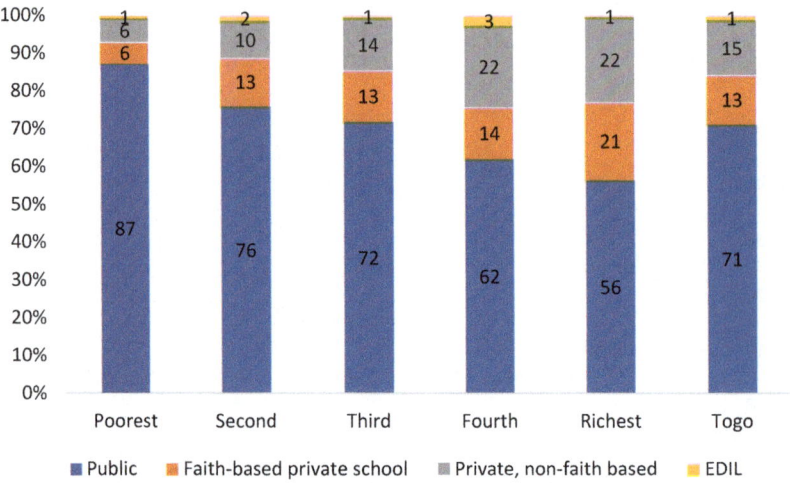

Fig. 5.2 School attendance by socioeconomic status (*Source* Authors' calculations using the 2015 QUIBB survey)

themselves—having the resources to pay for private education have a higher socioeconomic status (Fig. 5.2)—, are likely to be better educated themselves and may be more motivated to assist their children in the learning process, by offering an intellectually stimulating home environment and by engaging with their children in homework.

Schools clearly can benefit from a greater availability of inputs and Chapter 3 showed that this is likely to improve performance. Yet the root problem of poor learning outcomes has less to do with whether students go to a public or private school, or the availability of scholastic inputs (though they matter), and more with the quality of teaching. Teachers' knowledge is astonishingly low. Just to illustrate, only one in seven teachers is able to answer 70% of (grade 5) math or French questions correctly. In schools with the highest percentage of high-performance teachers, one in three teachers is able to do so. The quality of teaching is further affected by the reliance on assistant and temporary teachers (60% of the staff complement in public schools) and teacher absenteeism, which is astonishingly high. Absenteeism is highly correlated with being an assistant or temporary voluntary teacher, suggesting a relation with inadequate levels of pay. Indeed, the impossibility to recruit teachers of good quality and resorting to cheaper fixes seems to be one of the drivers of poor learning outcomes.

Adding a temporal lens to our reasoning, it is worth recalling that Togo did not always have a learning crisis (see Fig. 2.7) and that the crisis dates from before the abolishment of school fees. The learning crisis emerged in 2010 when PASEC tests scores showed a massive decline relative to those of a decade earlier. The majority of students in 2000 showed a satisfactory level of learning (around 70% of them in math in their fifth grade), while this percentage drops to 46% in 2010 and remains stable at that level thereafter. The decline cannot be attributed (solely) to the expansion of the school system, though, because students in grade 5 who had started their education career before free primary education was introduced also show a decline in learning similar to those in grade 2, who started after free primary education was introduced.

As the education system has been affected by multiple shocks, including the prolonged economic crisis, the large influx of additional students and the incorporation of EDIL schools into the public school system, it is difficult to assess whether teachers' knowledge declined because of adverse selection (the best teachers left), because unqualified teachers entered the system, or because increasing workload, and low pay, undermined teacher motivation. Irrespective of the cause, it is safe to conclude a massive effort is needed to (re)train teachers. Additional actions can be taken to improve learning, but these are likely to only improve outcomes at the margin: a better balancing of teachers and scholastic inputs across schools; stimulating parental involvement; reducing absenteeism and improving supervision.

Box 5.1 Community participation and school performance

Unsurprisingly given the high-value Togolese citizens attach to education, community participation at primary school level is almost universal, though the degree at which communities are active varies. Parents' associations and school management committee activities are mostly related to procurement and financial management (including bidding, supervision of works, reception and distribution of scholastic material, hiring of teachers, etc.) and less to monitoring school performance. Community participation has proven to be effective at reducing the costs of acquisitions, and a greater involvement of communities in monitoring school performance could be a catalyst for improved education outcomes. This is explored in Togo by the Data Must Speak initiative cofunded by the Global Partnership for Education, Hewlett Foundation and the UNICEF Thematic Fund for education.

Initial findings suggest that schools with higher community participation have a better health and nutrition environment (latrines, first aid kit, hand washing station, school canteen, nutrients distribution), more facilities (water, electricity, playground) and better learning conditions (textbooks, seats). Beyond the health/nutrition environment and learning conditions, community participation is also associated with more pedagogic activities, including teaching staff meetings and pedagogic support. This despite the fact that school management committees are not formally empowered to monitor school performance.

With respect to school performance, there are indications suggesting that higher community participation is associated with lower dropout rates and higher pass rates at the end of primary school national exam, even after controlling for the positive influence of a better endowed school on performance—echoing findings presented in Chapter 4.

Community participation can have an indirect (through improved health/nutrition and learning environment) as well as a direct effect on school performance

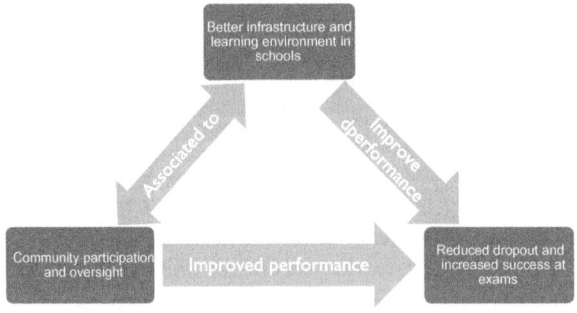

Source Personal communications data must speak initiative

5.2 What Can Be Done?

How can learning be improved? Even when there is agreement that a massive effort is needed to improve the quality of teaching, it is not immediately evident how to go about it. An important aspect is the realization that there is a stock and a flow problem. The stock problem refers to the existing cohort of teachers whose skills and teaching methods need to be upgraded. The flow problem refers to future teachers who have not yet entered the profession. Addressing the learning challenge requires different approaches for each group: the first group requires upgrading of their current skills, whereas the second group requires higher quality at entry in the profession. For this last group, it is somewhat simpler to envisage what is needed: greater selection at entry at teacher colleges and quality improvements of what is being taught at these colleges. This is not to suggest that the task is trivial. Higher quality individuals will need to be attracted to teacher colleges, with better salaries and better conditions, changes that will have major fiscal consequences. Then even if you are able to attract people with better qualifications and who are motivated to become teachers, they need to be equipped with proper pedagogical skills, requiring a retooling of existing teacher training institutes.

More challenging, however, is how to improve the quality of teaching by the existing cohort of teachers. Given the poor performance of these teachers on the learning tests, improving their skills is likely to be an important part of the challenge. But how to upgrade the skills of 25,000 teachers in the public school system (and 13,000 additional teachers in the nonpublic system), in ways that do not disrupt the school year and which are affordable? Many approaches can be envisaged. Just to mention a few: One could decide to invest in teacher cascade training. In the context of sub-Saharan Africa where limited resources often hinder efforts to improve teacher quality, cascade training is often seen as a preferred model of professional development for teachers. A cascade approach entails central training of a group of teachers as change agents who will pass on their new knowledge by training a large number of additional teachers. A cascade approach could be combined with regular teacher evaluations which are used to identify which teachers are most in need of retraining. Retraining could then focus on the bottom 10 or 20 percent (those who should not be in front of children teaching), while those who don't improve during the retraining program could be dismissed and replaced with higher quality, better trained teachers from the (retooled) teacher colleges.

Another approach could be the introduction of scripted instruction. This approach refers to teaching programs that have highly structured lessons, often with specific time allotments for teaching specific skills, and often word-for-word scripts of what the teacher is to say. Scripted instruction is advocated for schools where teachers have had inadequate teacher training and can be considered a way to standardize the quality of instruction. Critics say that such programs stifle teachers' creativity, undermine teachers' expertise, and fail to provide for the diverse needs of many classrooms. Advocates see it as the easiest way to provide teachers with the essential elements of effective reading instruction.

A fourth approach could be to introduce e-learning approaches, such as the flipped classroom concept. This is an approach that turns traditional teaching upside down. Instead of introducing concepts in class (by an under-skilled teacher) and then sending students off to do homework, students watch online or on preloaded tablet lessons prepared by expert teachers who introduce them to key concepts. Then students then use class time to tackle complex questions, working in small groups and under the supervision of their teacher.

All these approaches could help improve teaching in Togo, as could many other approaches including some which have been discussed in this book such as enhanced parental engagement, or a more equitable distribution of resources. Approaches could also be tried in combination. A cascade training can improve teacher skills and prepare them to use scripted lessons in their classroom. Scripted lessons can be combined with flipped classroom concepts. Flipped classroom approaches may be more suited for urban areas, where access to electricity (and the internet if this is needed) is more readily available, while scripted lessons may be more suited for rural areas.

The key point we'd like to emphasize is that it is not obvious from the outset which approach is most suited. Even impact evaluations, while essential in identifying the most promising approaches, are unlikely to give the necessary guidance as few will have been done in settings relevant to Togo. So, adopting one approach at the exclusion of others seems unnecessarily limiting. Why not start agnostically by agreeing that change leading to improved learning in the classroom is urgently needed while acknowledging that it is not evident what exactly needs to be changed. Next one could create an environment in which a systematic search for solutions is supported.

Such an approach would fall under what Andrews et al. (2012) call Problem Driven Iterative Adaptation or PDIA. They define four critical elements for approaches seeking solutions to complex problems, of which limited learning is one. These are:

1. aim to solve particular *problems* (learning in this instance) relevant to local contexts via
2. the creation of an environment that encourages experimentation and positive deviance, which gives rise to
3. active, ongoing and experiential (and experimental) learning and iterative feedback, doing so by
4. engaging broad sets of agents to ensure that solutions are viable, legitimate and relevant.

PDIA starts by asking—what is the problem, as opposed to defining the solution that should be adopted (step 1). Next teachers and headmasters but also parents or school inspectors should be given the space to define their own approaches and solutions (step 2). These will often entail adaptations to solutions that exist already, which is sensible given that local agents have a unique understanding of the problems at hand. Solutions are likely to be attained through incremental steps as few people are likely to get it right the first time. Muddling through needs to be accepted as part of the search process. It implies taking a gradual approach to addressing complex problems. Experimentation plausibly has its greatest impact when connected with learning mechanisms (step 3). These ensure the dynamic collection and immediate feedback of lessons about what works and why. Active learning through real-world experimentation allows reformers to learn a lot from the small step interventions they pursue to address problems (or causes of problems). They learn, for instance, about contextual constraints to change in general, how specific interventions work (or not), and how these interventions interact with other potential solutions. Finally (step 4), in order to translate workable solutions into permanent change in the system, broad sets of actors need to be engaged. The engagement is preferably to start from the beginning, as this creates a broad platform of people supporting the new approach, including parents, teachers, headmasters, school inspectors, etc.:

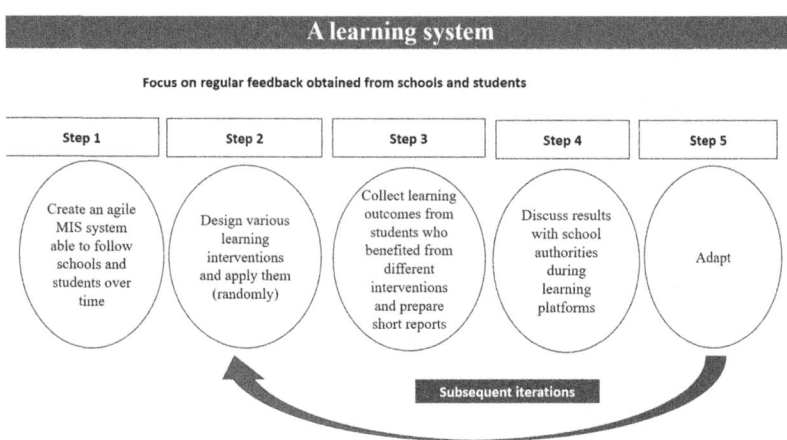

Togo is uniquely placed to adopt a PDIA approach to improve the pedagogical skills of the current as well as the future cohort of teachers. Togo's citizens and authorities have demonstrated to greatly care about education, investing significant private and public resources to ensure their students succeed. Togo's education system used to be a decent performer, suggesting that there exists institutional memory that can be tapped. Moreover, the education management information system in Togo is well developed and with adaptations suited to assess the impact of different experimental approaches. The management information system could also be complemented with other learning tools, such as Iterative Beneficiary Monitoring, which are light, cost-effective and have demonstrated to enhance learning by creating effective feedback loops.[2] And finally, Togo is at the sweet spot between not being too big to make experimentation a daunting task and being too small not to be able to do any real experimentation. With almost 5000 public schools, it pays to let different schools propose different approaches and experiment with them. Let some send their teachers to receive additional training; let others introduce scripted lessons; let a third group flip their classroom; let other schools propose their own innovations: more involvement by parents; classroom supervision by headmasters; school feeding;

---

[2] http://documents.worldbank.org/curated/en/377031522917012963/Iterative-beneficiary-monitoring-an-adaptive-approach-to-enhancing-the-implementation-of-World-Bank-projects.

a combination of teacher training and scripted lessons. Finally, do nothing in the nth group. Now let the system run for some time, maybe 2 years, maybe less, and analyze the results using quick tests and monitoring feedback. Use this to find the most promising innovation and repeat, now introducing variations of this innovation.

Reference

Andrews, Matt, Lant Pritchett, and Michael Woolcock. 2012. Escaping Capability Traps Through Problem Driven Iterative Adaptation (PDIA), CID Working Paper No. 240, June 2012.

The opinions expressed in this chapter are those of the author(s) and do not necessarily reflect the views of the International Bank for Reconstruction and Development/The World Bank, its Board of Directors, or the countries they represent.

Open Access This chapter is licensed under the terms of the Creative Commons Attribution 3.0 IGO License (https://creativecommons.org/licenses/by/3.0/igo/), which permits use, sharing, adaptation, distribution and reproduction in any medium or format, as long as you give appropriate credit to the International Bank for Reconstruction and Development/The World Bank, provide a link to the Creative Commons license and indicate if changes were made.

The use of the International Bank for Reconstruction and Development/The World Bank's name, and the use of the International Bank for Reconstruction and Development/The World Bank's logo, shall be subject to a separate written license agreement between the International Bank for Reconstruction and Development/The World Bank and the user and is not authorized as part of this CC-IGO license. Note that the link provided above includes additional terms and conditions of the license.

The images or other third party material in this chapter are included in the chapter's Creative Commons license, unless indicated otherwise in a credit line to the material. If material is not included in the chapter's Creative Commons license and your intended use is not permitted by statutory regulation or exceeds the permitted use, you will need to obtain permission directly from the copyright holder.

Correction to: Transforming Education Outcomes in Africa

Johannes Hoogeveen and Mariacristina Rossi

Correction to:
J. Hoogeveen and M. Rossi (eds.),
Transforming Education Outcomes in Africa,
https://doi.org/10.1007/978-3-030-12708-4

The original version of the book was inadvertently published as non-open access. It has been now changed to open access with Copyright Holder Name: © 2019 International Bank for Reconstruction and Development/The World Bank. The correction to the book has been updated with the change.

The updated version of the book can be found at
https://doi.org/10.1007/978-3-030-12708-4

© International Bank for Reconstruction
and Development/The World Bank 2019
J. Hoogeveen and M. Rossi (eds.), *Transforming Education Outcomes in Africa*, https://doi.org/10.1007/978-3-030-12708-4_6

Index

A
Absenteeism of teachers, 78
Academic skills, 88
Access to water, 35
Addition, 69–71
Africa Learning Barometer, 3
Africa's primary education system, 2
Analysis of variance (ANOVA), 76, 77
Analytical skills, 69
Assistant teachers, 37, 78, 80
Average years of schooling, 2

B
Basic infrastructure, 33
Book availability, 65, 78, 84

C
Cascade approach, 93
Cascade training, 93, 94
Causality, 39
Certificat d'études du premier degré (CEPD), 18, 36, 39, 40, 42, 43, 59, 60
Changes at the margin, 4, 82
Civil society, 88
Class size, 78
Commission nationale d'évaluation (CNE), 67
Community involvement, 4
Community participation, 91, 92
Complex problems, 95
Correlations among test scores, 71
Cost-effective, 96
Costs to schooling, 2
Cross-section, 48

D
Data Must Speak initiative, 92
Demand side, 5, 48, 80
Desk number, 45
Disadvantaged children, 88
Division, 69, 71
Donors, 10, 11, 20, 80
Drop out, 20, 25
Drop-out rates, 20, 44, 92

E

École d'Initiative Locale/local initiative schools (EDIL), 10, 14, 41, 80
Economic and political crisis, 23, 24, 91
EDIL schools, 10–13, 15, 20, 33, 91
Education, 1, 2, 4, 5, 10–13, 15, 18, 21, 22, 25, 26, 36, 37, 40, 52–59, 66, 79, 81, 83, 88, 90–92, 96
Educational opportunities, 47
Educational outcomes, 4, 33
Education quality, 3, 32
Education system, 4, 12, 13, 16, 22–24, 32, 58, 66, 91, 96
Efficiency, 4, 12, 16, 25, 31, 33, 36, 39, 59, 89
e-learning approaches, 94
Enrollment, 2, 4, 5, 11–13, 16, 23, 32–34, 48, 49, 53, 55, 56, 58, 64, 66, 88
Enrollment rate, 2, 4, 11, 44
Environment, 45, 59, 64, 67, 92, 95
Exam, 12, 13, 17, 18, 20, 36, 37, 39, 59, 64, 92

F

Family welfare, 82
Female teachers, 15, 79–81, 83
Fertility, 4
Financial constraints, 10
Flipped classroom, 94
Four basic operations, 69
Free education, 23, 80
Free primary education, 11–13, 15, 17, 20, 22, 25, 32, 65, 91
Free primary school reform, 2
Free universal education, 33
French, 3, 5, 10, 20, 22–25, 64, 65, 67, 68, 70–72, 74–83, 85, 88, 90

French vocabulary, 67, 68, 72
Frontier analysis, 31, 32, 42, 43, 59

G

Gap, 16, 17, 34, 35, 67, 79, 80
GDP growth, 18
GDP spending, 18, 88
Gender, 5, 12, 16, 22, 23, 25, 41, 44, 53, 56, 78
Global partnership for education, 92
Golfe-lomé, 34, 35, 39, 47, 72, 73, 75, 77
Government of Togo, 13, 14, 16–19, 21, 22, 38, 59
Grade four, 64, 67, 76, 88

H

Happiness, 4
Health, 5, 46, 48, 92
Health and nutrition, 4
Hewlett Foundation, 92
Home environment, 90
Homework, 94
Household composition, 5, 47, 48, 59
Household head, 47, 49, 53–55, 57, 59
Household surveys, 4, 40
Human capital, 64, 82

I

Inadequate learning, 87
Inefficiency, 32, 33, 42, 46, 59
Inequalities, 4, 12, 16, 17, 34, 36, 88, 89
Infrastructure, 45, 66, 67, 85
Innovation, 96, 97
Input, 15, 32, 33, 38, 39, 46, 59, 66, 80, 90
Intensive programs, 87
Intermediate proficiency, 3, 4

K

Key inputs, 67
Knowledge, 2, 5, 42, 64, 67, 68, 70, 73–76, 80, 84, 88, 93

L

Labor market, 4, 88
Latrines, 66, 92
Learning achievements, 20, 22, 24
Learning assessment survey, 64
Learning outcomes, 2–4, 20, 22, 32, 64–67, 79, 80, 82, 85, 87–91
Learning process, 90
Learning tests, 23–25, 93
Literacy, numeracy, and science, 2
Lomé, 5, 10, 16, 17, 37, 41, 46, 47, 52, 54, 56, 58, 70, 73
Low-income, 47
Low pay, 91

M

Management information system, 96
Marginal policies, 87
Maritime, 34, 36, 39, 46, 51, 56, 57, 75, 77
Mathematics, 3, 5, 20, 22–25, 44, 64, 67, 68, 70–83, 85, 88, 90, 91
Meetings, 79–81, 83
Micro data, 4, 88
Millennium Development Goal, 2
Mobile phones, 51, 53, 55, 57
Motivation, 32, 66, 89
Multiplication, 69–72, 75, 77
Multivariate analysis, 76, 78, 79

N

Non-verbal reasoning, 67–71, 73–75, 77, 78

Numbers, 68, 69, 75, 88
Nutrition, 92

O

Ordering number, 67, 68, 70, 71

P

Parental associations, 80
Parental background, 79
Parental choice, 82
Parents' associations, 83, 91
PASEC tests scores, 91
Pass rates, 12, 18, 25, 32, 40, 44–46, 92
Pedagogical skills, 74, 76
Pedagogic support, 92
Plateaux, 19, 35, 36, 39, 46, 47, 51, 56, 57, 70, 75–77
Policy suggestions, 87
Poorer households, 47, 88
Poor households, 17
Poor quality of teaching, 87
Population census, 40
Poverty map, 40
Primary enrollment, 2, 60
Primary school, 4, 10, 12, 13, 16, 17, 20, 23–25, 31–34, 36, 37, 39, 41, 50, 53–57, 59, 64, 67, 88, 91, 92
Primary school census data, 39
Primary school children, 5, 32
Primary school enrollment, 11, 13, 23, 33, 34
Primary school system, 3, 14–16, 24, 25
Private education, 10, 15, 24, 89
Private school effect, 79
Private schools, 5, 10–12, 15, 41–43, 45, 64, 70–72, 79, 82, 89, 90
Private school teachers, 12

Probit, 48, 49, 54
Problem Driven Iterative Adaptation (PDIA), 95, 96
Professional development, 93
Proficiency, 3
Proficiency in primary education, 3
Programme d'Analyse des Systèmes Éducatifs/Programme of Analysis of Education Systems (PASEC), 5, 17, 20, 23, 24, 32
Public education, 11, 13, 58, 88
Public investment, 82
Public primary education, 12, 88
Public provision, 10
Public schools, 10–13, 15, 16, 32, 33, 36–38, 42, 64, 66, 70, 71, 74, 80, 88–91, 93, 96
Pupil-teacher ratios, 66

Q

Qualifications of teachers, 4
Quality education, 4, 11, 23, 66, 67
Quality of schooling, 2
Quality of teaching, 90, 93
Quantity of schooling, 2
Questionnaire des Indicateurs de Base du Bien-être (QUIBB), 5, 32–34, 40, 48, 90

R

Reading comprehension exercises, 68
Real-world experimentation, 95
Reforms, 11, 12, 15, 16, 18, 21
Regional differences, 19, 32, 54, 56, 72, 75
Regional inequalities, 33, 58
Regression analysis, 39, 59, 78–81
Regressions, 39, 40, 42, 48, 53
Regressors, 42, 45
Rural areas, 2, 10, 12, 17, 41, 70, 72, 73, 75, 88, 94

S

Savanes, 10, 16, 17, 20, 32, 34–37, 39, 46, 47, 52, 55, 58, 70, 75–77
Scholastic inputs, 33, 35, 36, 66, 89–91
School fees, 2, 11–13, 15, 24, 65, 88, 91
School management, 4, 91, 92
School performance, 5, 32, 37, 38, 41, 44–46, 91, 92
School system, 3, 4, 9, 15, 22, 33, 80, 91
School year, 11, 13, 20, 24, 32, 93
Scores, 23, 64, 70–81
Scripted lessons, 94, 96, 97
SDI surveys, 59, 67
SDI test, 64, 68, 71, 75, 77
Shock, 13, 23, 33, 91
Slow growth, 13
Solutions, 95
Spending, 10, 18, 19, 25–27, 35–38, 88
Staff meetings, 92
Stochastic frontier, 31, 42, 46, 59
Student performance, 33, 64, 66
Students per classroom, 15, 23, 35, 36
Students per teacher, 15, 16, 35, 83
Student–teacher ratios, 11, 12, 16, 65, 66, 84
Sub-saharan africa, 3
Subtraction, 69, 71
Supply, 80, 82
Survey and Delivery Indicators (SDI), 5, 64–67, 71–77, 79–81, 84, 89

T

Teacher absenteeism, 32, 33, 90
Teacher experience, 45, 78
Teacher knowledge, 64–67, 84, 90, 91
Teacher motivation, 66, 80, 91
Teacher qualifications, 11, 64, 76, 78
Teachers, 5, 10, 11, 13–15, 22, 25, 33, 37, 38, 42–45, 59, 60, 64–67, 70, 73, 75, 76, 79–84, 89–91, 93–96
Teaching equipment, 65–67, 84
Teaching methods, 93
Teaching profession, 10
Temporary staff, 15, 66, 80
Temporary teachers, 15, 90
Test scores for teachers, 77
Textbooks, 20, 33, 65–67, 78, 79, 81, 83, 92
Togo, 3, 4, 10–12, 16, 18, 21–24, 32–34, 39, 47, 48, 59, 65–67, 75, 76, 80, 84, 88, 91, 92, 94, 96
Trade-off, 2
Train teachers, 91

U

UNICEF, 11, 92
Unqualified teachers, 66, 80, 91
Urban areas, 10, 17, 25, 42, 67, 72, 75–77, 83, 94

V

Variables, 40, 42, 45, 52, 53, 56, 58–60, 79, 82
Vocabulary, 68, 70, 71, 73, 75
Voluntary teacher, 37, 82, 90
Volunteer teacher, 15, 78, 79, 81, 83

W

Wages, 10
Wealth, 5, 23, 25, 33, 47, 58, 79
Wealth effect, 79, 82
West africa, 3, 10
West african countries, 11
Workload, 91
World values survey, 1

The manufacturer's authorised representative in the EU is Springer Nature Customer Service Centre GmbH, Europaplatz 3, 69115 Heidelberg, Germany. If you have any concerns regarding our products, please contact ProductSafety@springernature.com

Printed and bound by CPI Group (UK) Ltd, Croydon, CR0 4YY

23/03/2026

02076401-0004